The Historic New Orleans Collection
Monograph Series
Robert D. Bush, General Editor

*Observations
on the Colony of Louisiana
from 1796 to 1802*

Miniature of James Pitot (1761–1831),
painted in Paris in 1802

Observations
on the Colony of
LOUISIANA
from 1796 to 1802

BY JAMES PITOT

TRANSLATED FROM THE FRENCH,
WITH AN INTRODUCTION,
BY HENRY C. PITOT

FOREWORD BY ROBERT D. BUSH

Published for the Historic New Orleans Collection
by the Louisiana State University Press
Baton Rouge and London

Designer: Albert Crochet
Typeface: Linocomp Baskerville
Typesetter: Briarpatch Press
Printer and Binder: Thomson-Shore, Inc.

LIBRARY OF CONGRESS CATALOGING IN PUBLICATION DATA

Pitot, James, 1761–1831.
  Observations on the Colony of Louisiana from 1796 to 1802.

  (The Historic New Orleans Collection monograph series)
  Translation of the author's ms. titled: Observations sur la Colonie de la Louisiane de 1796 à 1802.
  Bibliography: p.
  Includes index.
2. Pitot, James, 1761–1831.   I.   Bush, Robert D.
II.   Title.   III.   Series: Historic New Orleans Collection. The Historic New Orleans Collection monograph series.
F373.P5713   976.3'03   79–14897
ISBN 0–8071–0579–1

Contents

Illustrations

Foreword

Several questions are posed by a historical memoir written in French by a naturalized American businessman living in New Orleans in 1802 on the topic of Spanish Louisiana at the time of the colony's retrocession to France. What was the origin of such a memoir? Who was its author? What purpose did it have? What effect, if any, did it produce? And, what value does such a memoir have for the historical literature of colonial Louisiana?

Bearing the imposing title *Observations sur la Colonie de la Louisiane de 1796 à 1802*, the manuscript comprises seventy-six handwritten pages of text. One intriguing aspect of the document is that the last six pages are in a different hand from that of the first seventy pages. In 1969 the authenticity of the *Observations on Louisiana* and authorship by James Pitot were proven by two New Orleans researchers. René J. Le Gardeur, Jr., and Henry C. Pitot published their conclusions in *Frenchmen and French Ways in the Mississippi Valley*, edited by John Francis McDermott (Urbana, 1969). Since that time, research efforts, despite the untimely death of Le Gardeur, have continued under the direction of Henry C. Pitot, a direct descendant of the author.

The *Observations* was originally composed by James (Jacques-François) Pitot in 1802, and was intended for

French officials with whom he hoped to establish official ties that would be of obvious benefit to his commercial enterprises in Louisiana. In addition to the text of the *Observations on Louisiana,* James Pitot also had two maps prepared by Barthélemy Lafon, well-known architect, surveyor, and cartographer of New Orleans. Tracings of these two maps have been discovered in the Archives du Service Historique de l'Armée at Vincennes. Also, a letter signed by Vice-Admiral Rosily was found in the Archives Nationales in Paris acknowledging Pitot's work. Additional substantial evidence confirmed the conclusion of Le Gardeur and Pitot attributing authorship to James Pitot. Although the two maps, reproduced as illustrations in this volume, are still available in France, the original James Pitot manuscript has been lost. Hence, the difference in the handwriting between the first seventy and the last six pages of the *Observations on Louisiana.* Obviously two different clerks copied the text translated here from the original document during Pitot's stay in Le Havre.

The manuscript has an almost draftsmanlike appearance, and remains very legible after more than a century and three-quarters. In the days before the typewriter, this kind of preparation of business reports was the only means of accurately recording governmental and business correspondence.

The manuscript copy was prepared originally in the office of Begouën, Demeaux and Company of Le Havre, a business firm with which James Pitot had dealings in 1802. Thereafter, the document remained in the family's archives until Maurice Begouën Demeaux allowed it to be examined by Le Gardeur. Several years after the death of Maurice Begouën Demeaux, his son Laurent gave the manuscript to Henry C. Pitot, who in turn donated it to The Historic New Orleans Collection. In this way, James Pitot's *Observations on Louisiana* has returned to a Louisiana repository where it can be used by researchers, and can become known by publication in this monograph series.

Originally, the manuscript was divided into several chapters, preceded by an introduction. Pitot's chapters, while still following his order, have been consolidated for purposes of clarity in presentation as follows: (1) government and finances; (2) police, judiciary, population, customs, and religion; (3) commerce; (4) agriculture; (5) trade with Indians; and (6) analytical topography. The six chapters are written in such a manner that the interrelationship between all of the subjects is still fully explained. James Pitot offers many firsthand examples of how these various subjects affected his daily conduct of business affairs in colonial Louisiana.

As a contemporary account the *Observations on Louisiana* has a great deal to tell us about conditions in Louisiana during the final years of Spanish sovereignty. To be sure, Pitot's work offers only the findings and conclusions of one individual, and one who did not have access to the reports and correspondence of Spanish officials. The manuscript is nevertheless extremely critical of the Spanish administration: "This colony of Louisiana—either through contempt, distrust, or ignorance of its worth, or in fact through politics, as I am convinced—has been kept in unmistakable isolation in its relations with the mother country and other Spanish possessions." At the same time, it does not hesitate to give credit where it is due, as in the case of its favorable assessment of Carondelet's term as governor.

James Pitot was one of those persons in 1802 who regarded Spain's policy toward Louisiana as dictated by her defensive priority for the more valuable properties in Mexico and Central America, which she intended to protect from Anglo-American, or French, intrusions that had already caused her no end of grief. At the same time, Pitot is quick to recognize the increasing power and territorial ambitions of the United States. He notes how its vitality and commercial expansionism constrasted so markedly with the lack thereof on the part of Spain and her officials.

The daily interaction between Spanish officialdom and the

Louisianians or foreigners resident in the colony is carefully described. Pitot presents the view of Spanish Louisiana that would be incorporated into the historical literature of the nineteenth century, especially by francophile historians such as Charles Gayarré. This view, in turn, has prompted a modern revisionist historiography, led by scholars such as Jack D. L. Holmes, which has sought to correct the "black legend": that is, the describing of all Spanish institutions in bilious language.

The *Observations on Louisiana*, translated into English and published for the first time, offers another important primary source of information on the conditions in colonial Louisiana prior to its purchase by the United States from France. The fact that James Pitot predicted such a possibility of American control in 1802, when the rumors of its transfer to France were being widely circulated, is indicative of the self-evident expansionism of the United States. "Perhaps Spain," Pitot concluded, "finally, will know what she ought to have done for the happiness and prosperity of this colony only when her lack of concern and the mistakes of her administration will have caused her to lose it."

James Pitot's final section, a topographical description of Louisiana, adds yet another dimension to the value of the *Observations*. Communications, transportation routes, portages, and geographical descriptions, collectively provide data with which to compare other contemporary accounts, and offer one more standard by which we can determine the relative utility of existing maps and charts. That the old maps and charts, antedating the Spanish administration, were still the only ones available for use by explorers and officials at this time serves as a reminder of the problems posed by distance, administration, and communications in Louisiana. The great expanse of territory designated as Louisiana seemed to defy, until the American explorations, accurate details in regard to distances.

James Pitot's credibility as a person from Louisiana to whom French officials paid heed is proven by the fact that Pierre Clément Laussat, colonial prefect and later commissioner of the French government, praised him. Daniel Clark wrote from London on October 22, 1802, that "a friend in Paris has written to me that Pitot has been introduced to the prefect, which gives me pleasure as he is capable of giving him important information." To what extent Pitot's *Observations* influenced French decision makers is not known, but his maps prompted both interest and correspondence.

In addition to the *Observations*, two appendices have been included by the editor because of their relevance to James Pitot's commentary. Appendix I is the verbatim text of the Treaty of San Lorenzo el Real (October 27, 1795), also known as Pinckney's Treaty. The privileged trading concessions, boundary lines, and the famous controversy that would emerge in 1802–1803 over the right of deposit (Article XXII) are discussed in detail by Pitot (the Americans, who enjoyed such privileges, were his competitors). Much of what James Pitot has to say regarding Spanish-American relations is illustrated in this treaty. The open door which it created for economic and political intercourse between the western United States and Louisiana was to have profound and lasting effects upon the people of both regions.

Appendix II is a list of tariff tables for the colony of Louisiana at the time of Pitot's arrival in Louisiana (August 24, 1796). His comments regarding the problems of doing business under the conditions outlined in the Spanish tariffs and duties can therefore be compared to the official schedule of import duties imposed by the government.

By 1796 when Spain was again involved in a European war as a foe of Great Britain, the American penetration of Louisiana was substantial, a fact of political reality symbolized by the Pinckney Treaty. Amid the resumption of European hostilities, with its obvious repercussions in the colonies, the

Spanish intendant, Juan Ventura Morales, issued both import and export tariffs in August of that year. Spanish commercial regulations were subject to changes and local interpretations throughout the years between 1796 and 1803, of which the most famous was the controversy in 1802–1803 begun with the Spanish cancellation of the Americans' right of deposit. Pitot's comments throughout this manuscript reflect the feeling of frustration with the apparent inconsistencies of Spanish commercial affairs and policy in Louisiana that were reflected in Spain's opening New Orleans to neutral shipping (1797–1798), and then restricting it (1799–1800). The tacit acceptance of American goods in Louisiana during wartime proved to be a great incentive to smuggling. Yet the tariffs remained a part of Spanish commercial policy, but seemingly with only arbitrary enforcement, and all of this caused several New Orleans merchants no end of grief and loss. Inclusion of the Spanish import tariff schedule for 1796 provides a great deal of information about the commercial interests of the colony and the monetary values for imports during this time.

Special thanks are due to several people who assisted in the preparation of this manuscript for publication. Mr. Benjamin W. Yancey was most helpful in his proofreading of the text. Dr. Jack D. L. Holmes carefully read the Spanish tariff schedule and offered his expertise in translation. Miss Maria J. Ybor diligently assisted in the typing of the Spanish and English text of the Pinckney Treaty.

Thus, James Pitot's *Observations* has been published, along with pertinent notes and appendices, in the hope of providing a useful source of information on the economic, political, and social conditions in Louisiana on the eve of its transfers in sovereignty from Spain, to France, and finally to the United States. It is indeed unfortunate that we do not have Pitot's commentary on similar subjects for Upper Louisiana, since he expressed the intention of writing it. However, the 1802 *Observations* constitutes one more piece of historical evidence in the never-ending search for documents about the history and heritage of Louisiana.

ROBERT D. BUSH

Translator's Introduction

When Spain accepted Louisiana from France in 1762, she did so reluctantly and in order to use it mainly as a colonial buffer zone between Spanish Mexico and England's colonies in North America. Louisiana, of secondary importance to the court of Spain because it lacked the mineral treasures of Mexico and South America, was considered a drain on the treasury and of little political importance in its own right. Among Louisianians, there was the feeling that Spain regarded the colony as a necessary liability in which her expenditures exceeded her revenues.

France had experienced the same unsatisfactory results prior to 1762, and yet there were Frenchmen who never understood why Louisiana had been ceded to Spain. They attempted to focus attention on the former French colony's merits and potential, in the hope of having it returned to her at some future time. However, not until the French Revolution did this movement receive any official support in Paris, and, at the same time, Spanish officials showed signs of a somewhat equivocal desire to part with Louisiana under the right conditions, which meant European properties. Late in 1795, and well into the following year, negotiations between France and Spain explored this possibility. Again in 1797 the subject was raised; but it was not until 1800 that any agreement to retrocede Louisiana to France was reached in the secret Treaty of San Ildefonso (October 1, 1800).

It was against this historical background that James Pitot, a New Orleans merchant and naturalized American citizen, wrote his *Observations on the Colony of Louisiana from 1796 to 1802*. Although news of the retrocession was very unofficial in both Paris and America, Pitot was convinced that it had been agreed upon. He therefore decided to go to France in May, 1802, in order to inform French officials of conditions in the colony and to present his *Observations* in the form of a report to the appropriate officials in the government and to members of the business community.

Baptized Jacques-François Pitot, though known as James in New Orleans, he was born in Villedieu-les-Poêles in Normandy, on November 25, 1761. When he was about twenty-one years old, he left France to settle in the French colony of Saint-Domingue in the West Indies, where he remained for the next ten years. Great fortunes were made during the late eighteenth century in this rich colony, but its overwhelmingly large slave population gave ominous indications of future trouble. In 1791 a slave revolt began on the great sugar plantations spreading rapidly across the whole of the island and particularly to Cap Français where James Pitot was living. Along with many of the Europeans in that area, Pitot returned to France and was thrust directly into a homeland undergoing its own great revolution.

During the Reign of Terror, which reached its bloody climax in France under Robespierre and the Jacobins in 1793–1794, Pitot attempted to return to Saint-Domingue. However, Cap Français was burned by the rebels before his ship could land, so he continued his voyage and eventually settled in Philadelphia, where he lived from 1793 to 1796 and became a naturalized American citizen. When Spain opened the commerce of Louisiana to United States citizens after 1795, James Pitot decided to go to New Orleans, which he did in 1796.

Shortly after his arrival in Louisiana, Pitot was named as a syndic (representative) on the local chamber of commerce. His selection to this position suggests that he quickly became recognized as one of the leading merchants of New Orleans. By 1800 he had built an imposing brick residence at 630–34 Royal Street, where he began work on his *Observations*. Further recognition of his influence in the business community of New Orleans is illustrated by his election as a ward commissioner just before his visit to France in 1802–1803. In March, 1804, he was appointed by the new American government to the city council, which then elected him as mayor of New Orleans in May of that year. James Pitot remained in that office for only a little over a year, when he resigned to give full attention to his increasing business affairs. In 1811–1812 he moved from his Royal Street residence to a new home on Bayou Saint John, now known as Pitot House and owned by the Louisiana Landmarks Society. In 1812 Governor William C. C. Claiborne appointed Pitot as the first judge of the newly created parish court of New Orleans, a post which he held until his death in 1831.

Because of his already extensive commercial experience and familiarity with civil law, James Pitot provides a useful commentary and analysis of Spanish policies during their waning years in colonial Louisiana. Highly critical of Spanish administrators during the years of his personal experience in Louisiana, he expresses some critical comments regarding their abilities, motives, and failures. He condemned the commercial policies of Spain most bitterly. Pitot blamed Spanish officials for the numerous ways in which they deliberately kept the colony from achieving any degree of prosperity in economic affairs, and inhibited the spirit of growth and the development of a sense of dignity among Louisianians. At the same time, he gives credit to the citizens of the western United States for their business energy after 1796, but he criticizes them for their carelessness and inexperience.

An ardent believer in the potential wealth and greatness of

Louisiana and for the prospects of the port of New Orleans, James Pitot predicted that Louisiana would one day rival any of the nations on the earth if its latent possibilities were properly recognized and administered. Only the Americans, he warned in 1802, seemed to envision the wealth and importance of Louisiana; and he predicted, even before the negotiations for the Louisiana Purchase began in Paris, that the United States would one day become its possessor.

In his comments on agriculture, James Pitot gives a comprehensive survey of the newly established sugar industry and of cotton production in Louisiana. In these observations, he drew upon his own experience with sugar in Saint-Domingue, where the industry had been one of the most successful in the world until its destruction by revolution. He is therefore able to make suggestions for improving the quality of Louisiana sugar, which offered the planters their first real opportunity for success—a concept, which according to Pitot, seemed totally alien to Spanish agricultural policies.

From his active participation in civic affairs in New Orleans, James Pitot provides some pertinent observations on such topics as religion, customs, race relations, trade with the Indians, and geography. He gives an extended commentary on police supervision and judicial proceedings in New Orleans.

The concluding section on topography consists of a long and comprehensive description of Lower Louisiana, as well as comments about two detailed maps, copies of which have been included with the *Observations on Louisiana*. Unfortunately, his topographical survey comes to an abrupt end just as Pitot begins his description of the region of Upper Louisiana. Whatever the reason for its sudden ending, the existing manuscript constitutes an important document in the annals of the last years of European control in Louisiana.

Several persons played an important role in the publication

of these *Observations.* Among them were: Maurice Begouën Demeaux of Le Havre, eminent scholar and historian, who originally owned the manuscript; Gabriel Debien of Paris, a leading authority on the former French colony of Saint-Domingue, who first recognized the importance of this document; and, of course, René J. LeGardeur, Jr., prominent New Orleans historian and researcher. Most important, however, were the encouragement and support of my wife Anita, without which this English translation might never have been completed.

HENRY C. PITOT

Observations
on the Colony of Louisiana
from 1796 to 1802

Introduction

If circumstances make it possibe for me to publish my *Observations on Louisiana*, I expect that there will be many opposing views, especially among those who, misled by the information they have received regarding this part of the New World upon visiting it, have experienced only boredom, privation, and misfortune.[1] Others, in traveling through the remote regions of the United States, have seen only the sparsely populated banks of the Ohio, and the flat and muddy banks of the Mississippi. Then there are those who, having reached New Orleans, have wanted to see only its present resources, without seeking to ascertain the real origins of its mediocrity. And, finally, some visitors have become frightened by the unhealthiness of a land whose disadvantages have been aggravated and perpetuated by the government's indifference and neglect.

I do not conceal at all that these observations have a mark of imperfection about them, for which I would not have the right to claim indulgence if I prided myself on being a man of letters; but carried along by the nature of my work far from the studies which develop one, I shall offer them just as they are written.[2] I should have liked to abstain from describing the administration's faults in such detail, but I do not believe it possible for me to avoid it. I must respond to the argument often made against Louisiana, in citing that France had ceded it only because she had recognized the impossibility of making something out of it, and that for a period of thirty years the wealth of Spain had not been able to free it from misery.[3] More than any other colony, Louisiana has experienced the extent to which a government could go in tying up its resources; yet Louisiana will soon prove that the combined advantages of its situation can overcome the most malevolent authority. This consideration has expressly made me go into details which sometimes might seen inconsequential, but which, when multiplied many times over in the operation of the government, have largely occasioned that stagnant mediocrity that made other nations prudently look with disfavor on ownership of Louisiana.

I am not writing these *Observations* for personal gain, but based upon rumors of the retrocession of Louisiana to France, I intend to present them respectfully to the government of its mother country as if it were indeed retroceded, or at least to make them known to businessmen who might be interested in commercial projects which I shall submit.[4] I have done everything that was expected of me to know the truth. I have omitted those matters for which I have not obtained at least virtual certainty; and if by chance my criticisms of the government seem to be exaggerated, I can only refer to the approval which, I believe, any impartial resident or traveler will give them. Be that as it may, let no one identify me with the preachers of insurrection; I would be ashamed to be compared to them.[5]

The errors of the Spanish government in Louisiana are those that perpetuate the mediocrity of a country, but which individually do not bother its citizens. Such an administration restrains commerce, restricts population, and does not encourage agriculture; and, by this unchanging policy, as well as the mingling of Spanish families with French ones, it has hardened an indifference in the colony that scarcely suspects the possibility of a better existence. Finally, the administration is, in fact, often arbitrary and corrupt, but most of the inhabitants are, nevertheless, peaceful and perhaps content in their mediocrity. Several persons, probably no more concerned but certainly more discerning, have reflected, like me, on the causes that have retarded and still are retarding the prosperity of this colony.[6] And if it is likely that a true account of Louisiana's situation and resources can make the government owning it give closer attention to its needs, it is none the less certain that a revolutionary upheaval would cause its ruin.

When I arrived in Louisiana in August, 1796, all existing circumstances indicated to me that the colony was in a distressed state. Its languishing commerce was expiring under the weight of an exorbitant tax and from restraints which continually endangered its existence. Its debt-ridden planters and completely ruined agriculture—the result of either the weather's uncertainty, destructive hurricanes, or the fury of a river which during five or six months every year threatens to swallow up all the inhabitants along its banks— foretold a total ruin. As much for the despair of the newcomer, as to curb the activities of the older residents and to hide from their view the wealth which the future promised them, political opinions which the government repressed or favored, guided by its self-interest, had in fact poisoned the populace who, through imitation, became in general either partisans of an obnoxious tyranny, or zealous adherents of Robespierre and the disrupting monsters who shared his crimes.[7] The planter who was in comfortable circumstances through luck, or by savings from his previous crops, already shared the anxieties of those whose ruin was complete. The businessman, whose efforts in better times had been crowned

3

with success, placed his capital in the sparse remnants of a commodity which the soil had almost refused to produce: indigo.[8] And both of them, blinded by the situation in which France then found herself and surely by divine inspiration of what she is now experiencing, either looked toward their native land which they wished to see again at peace, or recalled to mind its government, hoping to obtain from it alleviation of their troubles.[9] Such was the state of affairs which existed in Louisiana when I arrived there in August, 1796.

After this description, one will no doubt be surprised to find me attempting to write about a country whose condition has not yet undergone any improvement, and whose possessions and tranquility, in most respects, have often been jeopardized by the policy of a government which could find, in its kindness and its self-interest, reasons to have made it already enjoy the prosperity that the future in large part promises. It will be astonishing, I say, that I should rescue Louisiana from oblivion, and, I would dare say, from the kind of contempt in which it is held among the group of colonies which Europeans have established in the West Indies. That is, nevertheless, the objective that I now set for myself in my *Observations*. Written with both truthfulness and impartiality, they are the result of five years of reflection on this province; and, they are inspired by my wishes that colonial government by France will hasten to bring Louisiana out of the condition of nothingness to which it has long been condemned only by a conduct, all the more ill-advised, on the part of Spain which has not, up to now, taken any of the necessary steps to maintain it.[12] I do not pretend to give here the complete history of Louisiana. It would be tedious to repeat the particulars of its listless progress during the many years since its discovery; and although several other authors have written about it in detail, the more renowned have, in their comprehensive surveys, refuted Louisiana's lack of

4

productivity which I myself should also like to prove.

Situated on a continent which generally appeared to the adventurers who discovered it as being one of a most savage nature, Louisiana provides very little of interest in the narration of its history. Similar in a way to Egypt, in its floods, climate, products, and fertility, in antiquity it was neither the cradle of the arts and sciences that have enlightened the world, nor the storehouse of a commerce as valuable as it was rich, which exposed Egypt to so many revolutions, and which has recently made it of great importance in European affairs.[11] Always uncivilized and listless in the past, the present begins to smile on Louisiana, and the future should make it a flourishing colony.

I shall not further distract the reader's attention by long recitations, or new stories, about the Indians who still occupy a part of these lands. In general ignorant and barbaric throughout America, they nearly all resemble one another in their morals and habits; and to arouse curiosity regarding them it would be necessary, like so many others have done at the expense of truth, to embellish some events about which even tradition gives no indication. A little more rational and more provident than the animals of the forests, less modest, and generally filthier than they are, they had, and often still have, all of their ferocity. If among the viciousness of their customs, some fine examples of sensibility and courage are often observed, it is, nevertheless, true that someone like myself, who has visited several Indian tribes, or who has been able to talk with reliable travelers about those things of which he has no knowledge, finds everywhere the repulsive ridiculousness of their morals, the horror or futility of their religious ceremonies, the barbarism of their politics, and finally that veneer of bestiality which often makes an Indian seem hardly better than part civilized and part tiger.[12]

Thus, in writing these *Observations* I shall barely mention the past, as to which my comment is, I believe, incontestable. I shall be satisfied, as to most recent events, to speak only about those which can throw some light on the present condition of Louisiana. Rarely, in touching on the different aspects of government, shall I refer to what preceded my arrival, and I shall end by offering my readers conjectures regarding the future.

CHAPTER ONE

Government and Finances

Others before me have successfully demonstrated the influence that these first two divisions of administration have on those which are subordinate to them, and more particularly on commerce and agriculture.[1] The observations that I shall present first on government and finances are not, so to speak, just exceptions to those that I shall have occasion to mention while referring later to all the other administrative branches of the colony.[2] I shall, perhaps, even be so clumsy as to repeat myself sometimes, but I thought this preliminary outline necessary in order to give an idea at the outset of their moral influence and of Louisiana's political situation.

Before beginning these *Observations*, I think it necessary, in order to justify the kind of bitterness with which I shall express myself, to warn that I intend to speak only about the government in the province of Louisiana, and that nothing I say in my *Observations* is written to reflect on the character of the Spanish nation. Never having traveled in any other Spanish possession, in general I want to speak only about what I know; and I seek, finally, to permit myself to judge only by my own experience, and not on the basis of reports sometimes basically true, but nearly always exaggerated or even embittered in their content.

The colony of Louisiana—either through contempt, distrust, or ignorance of its worth, or in fact through politics, as I am convinced—has been kept in unmistakable isolation in its relations with the mother country and the other Spanish possessions. And I am inclined to believe that this colony's administration, in its vices and errors, has the same mark of isolation. After that expression of my views, I now go on to commence the *Observations*, which should result in my giving a statistical summary of the province of Louisiana. But it pains me to have more often only mistakes or corruption to criticize, and to be able to focus Europe's attention on it only by an almost continuous disapproval of a policy that reason and self-interest condemn, and abuses which make the results more pernicious.

The first reproach which one could make against the government, and which contrasts strangely with the opinion that one generally has of Spanish pride, is its lack of dignity, not only in the functions where law and authority call for it, but also, I would dare say, in the abuses which officials make of it. A governor general of Louisiana does not limit himself to the duties which, keeping him at a distance from most of the population, would maintain for him that dignity so necessary in the colonies. The minute details of police administration are carried on by him daily; in being present at the hearings he attends to a large number of people who should only be dealt with by police officers under his supervision. Moreover he devotes to unimportant local problems of his government the time and attention which he owes to a vast colony in need of so many improvements.

From this variety of duties performed by the principal head of a colony, arise many of the disadvantages harmful to his administration. Excessive arrogance provokes hatred among those governed; too much popularity often breeds contempt. A governor general should always know how to find a happy medium in order not to lose any of his dignity, yet by giving daily hearings to trivial or immoral police matters, which he should know about only from the reports of minor officials, how can he flatter himself as being able to render equitable judgments in all cases? In such an event, how could he instill in the hearts of the punished or the condemned a realization of their crimes? Indeed, half of the accused in this situation (being summoned before a governor general), thinking that they have acquired the right to plead, show an attitude humiliating to the individual and harmful to authority. If, on the other hand, a chief of state knows how to govern in his own name by a strict and businesslike supervision, he has only the quarrels of his subordinates to answer for, the consequence of which will not reflect upon him. It is in his name that the victim of oppression has obtained justice. It is to him that the condemned person would have wished that his case had been submitted. It is to his tolerance that the guilty would have wanted to resort, and his authority is all the more respected, as he has less occasion to use it personally.

A second reproach, which an experience of five years justifies my making against the government of Louisiana, is that it is not understood in community life, at least in a manner to gain the respect of that portion of the population which, because of its customs, economic status, and education, is practically ignorant of the effects as well as the aims of the discussions concerning the police supervision to which I have referred above.[3] One never sees around the governor that frequent and desirable gathering of a select group of estimable men which confidence would attract; instead, only those appear who are called there by duty despite themselves. Some flatterers among the residents, some adventurers among the foreigners, are mainly those constantly welcomed; and a governor general, who has become indifferent even to the military whose rank more closely approximates his, appears in the eyes of the entire colony only as a menacing lictor armed with the fasces of authority, and not as the benevolent leader, dispenser of the king's bounties and patronage.

The third reproach to be made against the government of Louisiana is one that is unfortunately common to most: venality. I do not believe that there is a country in the world where duty to the sovereign is more shamelessly transgressed, and where there is hardly any secrecy in the selling of favors among those in a position to do so. Citizens of all classes buy for hard cash what equity, merit, or services rendered should enable them to enjoy freely. A privilege, a command, a permit to trade with the Indians, costs either a quadruple payment, or an allowance to the governor and the secretary, or the cancellation of a legitimately contracted debt. And finally, to fill the cup to the brim, immoral establishments pay bribes to be protected from interference by minor police officials.

Although I do not believe that I can be accused of exaggeration, since at times a nobler spirit on the part of the governor could eradicate the vicious conduct spread throughout the colony, I do not say that there were no exceptions. Without either excusing or blaming those who governed the colony before my arrival, and allying myself with the tradition that does not spare them reproach, I shall specifically exclude M. de Carondelet, who was governing when I arrived in Louisiana, from the charge of venality.[4] He is also worthy of being exonerated from the first reproach that I made against the government; his unruffled self-control when considering police matters, his personal investigations and his efforts to be able to judge with full knowledge of the facts, surrounded him always with a respect that brought the reputable citizens closer to his presence. I should like to be able to exonerate him completely from the second reproach, as he should be from the charge of venality, but I am obliged to acknowledge that in the manner in which he arranged his private life, he sometimes gave an example that has only too often been imitated and perhaps causes even today that kind of distrust and withdrawal by the citizens from contact with their leaders. This circumstance regenerates or perpetuates abuses to which Carondelet himself was a stranger, and which closer relations and contacts might perhaps have restrained. It was actually the weak side of his administration's routine, and in viewing the entire matter impartially, these faults should be attributed to the critical circumstances under which he took over the government of the province. Because of war times and the revolution [in France], Carondelet was compelled to fear public disorders which he himself perhaps exaggerated, and to avoid men who were daily represented to him as seditious, and against whom he often thought that he was on the verge of having to take up arms.[5]

The colony was barely emerging from these fears when I arrived. The treaty of peace between France and Spain removed any motives for distrust on the part of the government.[6] The intended expedition for the conquest of Louisiana, led by the French representative to the United States, was more than ever imaginary, and the citizens whom Carondelet had thought necessary to treat severely were back in their homes.[7] But if the causes no longer existed, it was not so regarding the effects. People were still embittered. They could not forgive the measures which the government had thought necessary to adopt for its own protection. Through hatred, the majority of the population still spurned, or held aloof from, the few who had aligned themselves with the measures taken by Carondelet. They remembered an incident when the cannons of the forts were ready to be aimed at the city; they talked about the deportation and treatment of several French patriots; and, they did not forget the step that they had suspected the government of taking in preparing to reinforce itself against the whites with the help of the free people of color.[8] They cited the proofs, true or false, of the complicity of this very government in the insurrection of the Pointe Coupée Negroes.[9] They thought themselves surrounded by treacherous spies who, through their activities, had compromised the serenity and wealth of many citizens. And, finally, they saw in the treaty of alliance between Spain and France, only the necessity on the part of Spain to yield, for the time being, to the superior arms of France, and the formal and secret intention [by Spain] to seize the first opportunity for vengeance that would extend as far as the population of Louisiana.[10]

In order to reach a reasonable conclusion regarding this quarrel between the government and its citizens, it would be necessary for an impartial observer to obtain from both parties admissions that might account for their mistakes and show them the error of their ways. Then also to find out from the citizen—forgetting that he was Spanish and not French—to what extent he has applauded in his public or secret assemblies, by his actions, and in his correspondence, a revolution that Spain opposed by force of arms. Finally, to ascertain to what point, manifesting his hopes for his former fatherland, he has justified the Spanish government's uneasiness and threats. If, on the other hand, it had been possible to obtain from Carondelet the orders that he had received from the court, the records verifying the plans of the French legation in the United States for the invasion by way of the Ohio River, and the reports of his spies on the collusion of the inhabitants with the enemy, to acquire evidence of their schemes concerning rebellion in favor of France, and, finally, to submit to a truthful examination all the official papers of the government's secretariat relative to this alarming situation and the circumstances of the insurrection that took place among the Negroes, then a sentiment of reciprocal forbearance could possibly erase from all minds the bitter memories. A spirit of understanding might then have led to congratulating one's self on having had as governor at such a time a man of French origin who, in fulfilling his duties as a Spaniard, committed few errors where another might have resorted to violence.

Carondelet did a great deal for commerce, or wanted to do so, particularly when he was intendant or governor.[11] I would venture to say that circumstances impeded his hopes for agriculture, as he made some efforts to encourage it, either by granting concessions of land, or by reaching several decisions that could increase the population, or by seeking to procure seeds for the areas that were suitable for grain crops. The orders of the court, or his fears, led him to employ money and labor for the building of imposing forts, money which the colony could have put to much better use. But, if he was wrong on this score, or had a task to fulfill, one can hardly deny him the justice of admitting that, under the general subject of maintaining order in the colony and improving its waterways, he started some projects, or provided several models, that are today only in ruins or neglect.[12] I shall, nevertheless, not blame the indifference that the present government showed in maintaining the costly fortifications with which Carondelet needlessly surrounded New Orleans. I would decry, however, the neglect of the roads, bridges, and levees; the relaxing of police regulations which he supervised more carefully; and the carelessness in failing to continue to maintain the work that Carondelet was hardly able to point out for drainage of the city's outlying sections, and for the development of navigation on the lakes.

Finally, I shall venture to render justice to Carondelet for the manner in which he had looked upon the province of Louisiana. Its political value was, above all, perfectly well known to him, and if he foresaw the importance that the western states of the United States would one day be to the commerce of New Orleans, he did not miss any occasion to influence them in favor of his mother country. The French Revolution that kept him from objecting to all of the measures initiated by many of his predecessors also largely favored the treaty which, by reestablishing the former English territorial boundaries, frustrated his plans and projects for the moment.[13] Soon recalled to a more lucrative government post, but perhaps less interesting politically speaking, Carondelet left Louisiana after having been able to outline some improvements there, and departing with none of those unanimous regrets which different times would have assured him.[14]

A new governor finally took charge of the colony; and it was under him that the article of the treaty between Spain and the United States, which ceded to the latter the left bank of the Mississippi as far as the thirty-first parallel, was put into effect.[15] Carondelet—as a clever politician and knowing the general value of the province of Louisiana to the court of Spain, perhaps even for the European powers who wanted to hold on longer to their colonies—eluded this cession as long as he could, well convinced, as his experience had shown him, that it was better to avoid compliance than to expose one's self to being eventually conquered. It is to be assumed that some very compelling circumstances forced the Spanish court to agree to boundaries that brought ambitious neighbors to the gates of New Orleans, and, without any advantage for Spain, established their access to the mouth of the Mississippi.[16] Those who gave some thought to this step foresaw all its consequences. Others saw in it an indifference on the part of the court towards this colony, confirming the already widespread rumor of a secret article in the treaty [Treaty of Basel of July 22, 1795] with France by which Louisiana was retroceded to its former rulers. Spain, in that case, was not making any real sacrifice, and the United States seemed to approve her conduct while awaiting full possession of Lower Louisiana, which they cannot fail to covet since it will keep their western states in submission. Lower Louisiana is the unique key and, consequently, the only obstacle to their ambitions in this part of the New World.

It was under this new governor [Gayoso] that many ill-advised or injurious steps were taken with respect to the routine of the former administration. Familiar with the needs of the colony and the character of its inhabitants as a result of the long period he had lived in Louisiana, one could expect from his knowledge a plan of development which the colony needed. But, poor and in debt, his needs often took precedence over his duties. His quarrels with the intendant brought about measures or compromises that benefited neither agriculture nor commerce, and his partiality for the United States, too strong not to be suspect, deprived him of all claims that he might have had to public confidence. The treaty with the United States [1795] had exacted a settlement in favor of commerce which broke several links in the Spanish government's chain of control in Louisiana, and it became a cover for the means that free access to the Mississippi gave the United States to ruin the local speculator by smuggling, and to deprive the intendant of customs duties.[17] And a senseless act on the part of the intendant concurred in furthering the interests of the United States: their ships alone were allowed to enter the port by paying only the duties required of Spanish nationals, whereas this measure ought to have been extended to all neutral vessels in order to settle in New Orleans a population foreign to the United States, and not solely to attract [American] neighbors whose number multiplies rapidly and becomes a sort of taking over in advance. Spain would then have established there the foundations of a population that Europe could one day take under its protection, and they would not have sacrificed national interest to culpable [population] exclusions, misconceived and harmful.

Without the circumstances [Convention of Môrtefontaine, September 30, 1800] that have reestablished peaceful relations between France and the United States, Spain would perhaps already have regretted that she did not adopt to the fullest extent the means at her disposal to make of New Orleans a city as powerful through its resources as it is worthy of respect in its population.[18] During the war it might have been a storehouse for the supplies of Mexico; Spain would have been more politic in that regard than she was in opening Vera Cruz and other ports to Anglo-American vessels, and perhaps she had lost sight of the fact that if there is a people on the globe today whom she should fear to admit into the ports of Mexico, it is indeed those of the United States.[19]

The government was soon disturbed by the inevitable consequences of the cession to the United States of new boundaries on the Mississippi. Menaced by a break in relations with the French that could not avoid causing one with Spain, the United States plotted to assure Lower Louisiana for themselves by a surprise attack. It was a political measure and necessary to avoid any further apprehension regarding their western states, whose vain efforts at rebellion in order to gain exclusive possession of the mouth of the Mississippi would thereby be frustrated.[20] Under the pretext of up-risings among the Indians and the landing of munitions and soldiers by the French on the Florida coast to help them, the United States recruited the little army in their eastern states which they rapidly moved into the Mississippi Territory [1798], and with which they destined to make Spain regret her culpable policies toward the province of Louisiana. In this manner they acted on expectations, all the more justified as perhaps I shall not exaggerate too much in saying, that the colony found itself half surrendered because of its situation to the person [James Wilkinson] whom Spain bribed several years before to condition favorably the sentiments of the Kentucky inhabitants, and governed by the man who, when he held a lesser rank, disseminated the irresistible oratory and arguments of desertion.[21]

By reciting these events, virtually proven in the eyes of all observers, I do not flatter myself that I have unimpeachable proofs in my possession; but in addition to agents and the eyewitnesses to many of these intrigues who have given me details confidentially, it is a fact that I was in the Natchez country in 1798, when the recruits and the general of the little army arrived.[22] Many questions were put to me then on the state of affairs in New Orleans, and many inconsequential conversations took place in my presence among those who thought it richer than it really is. I traveled at the same time among Indian tribes who, far from rising up against the United States, were rather under that country's orders. In the western states, and especially in Kentucky, I heard discussed a hundred times the issue of the conquest of Louisiana, against which there was a majority in Kentucky, who, by preventing recruitments, made themselves suspect to the others. I visited Philadelphia, New York, and Baltimore under similar circumstances, where it was a crime to be a Frenchman.[23] Finally, I read in the newspapers about the imaginary tale of the landing of French brigands on the Florida coast, and many other stories invented to serve as an answer to the responsible citizens of the United States who rightfully asked: Why then an army? Why so many useless expenditures by the government? Show us the enemy we must repulse. Apart from the fact that I saw and heard all that is described above, and many other things useless to report here, I shall say again that there is perhaps not an intelligent man in New Orleans who after what was taking place has not followed my example in repeatedly saying to his friends: There is talk about a United States army that is assembling in the Natchez district to come and seize Lower Louisiana. But do you not believe that in the absence of Louisiana's measures and preparations for resistance, the United States can regard it as its own property?

Fate decided otherwise. France and the United States not having engaged in open warfare, and thus having no pretext to justify a break in relations with Spain, the little army disbanded without having been able to undertake anything. And chance thus ordained that having been a witness to its formation during the course of my travels, I was present at its disbandment, for it was leaving the Spanish frontier when I passed through Natchez on my return.[24] Wilkinson, its general, came to New Orleans several months later in order to see his old friend, the governor general of the province. He was lodged and entertained at the governor's home, but the toasts to their joyful reunion were repeated so often that as soon as Wilkinson departed for the United States, a malignant fever ended Gayoso's career.[25]

The political crisis which I have just described was not the only one that threatened Louisiana, for at the same time another was in preparation which did not escape the surveillance of Chevalier d'Urujo [Mariano Luis Urquijo] Spanish Ambassador in Philadelphia, and which finally failed, having involved only spies, couriers, and letter writing. Its center of activity was also in the United States, under the direction of Colonel or General Blount, but it was in the interest of the British government.[26] The alleged armament of French brigands, who were supposed to furnish weapons, munitions, and soldiers to the Indians, was invented only to cover up those measures which the British *themselves* were preparing and which they entrusted, as the outcome would seem to indicate, to one of their former fellow citizens living as an Indian for many years among the Creek Nation. This man named [William Augustus] Bowles had been deported to Europe by the Spanish government for having already caused trouble, and I shall have occasion to speak later about his arrival and his delayed and unsuccessful efforts.[27]

A particular event might have favored either one of these plots, as a *cédula*, or royal order, dated April 20, 1799—to which I shall refer in my observations on commerce—might have arrived thanks to the slowness or uncertainty of the European mail destined for the colonies, at the time of the attack upon Louisiana, if it had taken place. This order prohibited Louisiana from using the only means that its particular situation afforded to import supplies or export its commodities. What kind of argument had justified the need for such an order? Would the Louisianians in a state of destitution and abandon, and for a fatherland that sustains this province only in a sort of precarious adoption, have preferred fighting to peace, misery to abundance, chains to freedom? And to assure themselves at that time of supplies as rich as they are abundant, and the exportation of all the colony's products, would not the farmers, businessmen, and citizens of all classes have joined with the enemy rather than expose themselves to the dangers of a decree, the success of which would have driven out of the province those [the Americans] who alone could have brought it to life and furnished it with supplies?[28] Spain would have then begun to realize her failures and errors with respect to the means of retaining Louisiana, and England or the United States would soon have convinced her of its importance.

More than two years of interim government followed the death of the governor general, and that provided an example of the confusion into which the Spanish government falls. At the outset, and for several months, a number of commanding officers, of equal rank in the service of the province, made known their claims to take over temporarily the military affairs under the title of commandants. Civil government and police supervision was assumed by the military counselor who is normally only the governor general's consulting attorney. This arrangement, which the Spanish laws ordained, created a third executive, the effect of which was to place shackles on the business of government by claiming to take advantage of, or usurping, certain rights and prerogatives. As a result, there is more arrogance in the intendant's office, dilatoriness in the courts, and more provocation in the military command where often an officer, who has spent his life in the service of the colony, cannot do the good which he knows is urgently needed, and who, in strengthening the esteem and confidence of his fellow citizens, would also merit for himself the gratitude of the court.[29]

A governor then arrived whom the captain general of Havana commissioned as interim commander of the armed forces.[30] I shall certainly have occasion to give an idea of his character in my observations on commerce; but in several circumstances the colony had to express its satisfaction that he took a more active role than the law accorded him—first of all in the protests regarding the royal *cédula* of April 20, 1799, which I have just mentioned, and then, as will be seen, with respect to the importation of Negro slaves which the intendant nevertheless had the power to thwart.

It was during the military government of Casa Calvo that Bowles—European by birth, Indian by profession, who had escaped from the pursuit of the Spaniards and was finally employed by England—arrived on the Florida coast with weapons, gifts, and munitions in order to induce his Indian brothers to declare war against the Spaniards. He had been up against delays and adversities which had led him to Jamaica. There he had gathered together a kind of general staff. But much greater misfortunes awaited Bowles on the shore, and a shipwreck cast him on the beach with all his followers, after he had jettisoned the most essential items in his armament.[31] Advance sentry of a British foray, he had a short-lived success in taking from the hands of a coward the fort of the Apalachee Indians, but soon repulsed by the forces that the Spanish military commander sent against him, he fled to the haunts of the tribe to which he had been attached for so long. His secretary with one of his lieutenants —young men deceived by that adventurer whom England would have acknowledged only after some great victories— were only too glad to find refuge in the colony.

The arrival of a governor general finally ended the temporary appointments in the military and civil departments, and it is with the beginning of his official duties that I end my observations on the government, so as not to repeat myself too much on that which I shall have occasion to present later.[32] The interim military commandant—whose fits of anger and partiality had made the colony apprehensive lest the king might have appointed him governor general, and who, better informed than he had been when he first arrived, may not have governed as badly as one might have feared— departed. Soon there was a renewal and even an expansion of the routine and venal ways of a continually vicious administration. That commandant [Casa Calvo] either through wealth or pride, or even principle, had not been corrupt; but an old man [Manuel de Salcedo] near the end of his life— infantile, poor, almost paralyzed, angered by family reverses —sought to profit in his old age from the advantages which his position gave him, and in combining frequent abuses of his military authority with maneuvers of financial pilferage, took advantage of all the circumstances to put an end, a bit late as a matter of fact, to the adversities of fate in his regard. Privileges and commissions were confirmed; changes were made in the commercial auctions; and the prohibition of importing slaves was maintained without any political, rural, or commercial advantage. That government will go from bad to worse.

I come now to the question of finances, about which I cannot say very much without the risk of repeating myself, as the close connection between commerce and finances forces me to reveal later on the corruption and errors of its conduct in this regard. An intendant is the chief financial officer and from his tribunal rise up that swarm of extortioning tax collectors that Spain pays to become themselves the instigators of a contraband trade as culpable for them as it is degrading for the smuggler. Depraved by gold that they covet, they also spread corruption among the merchants, and becoming in turn informer of one and the accomplice of the other, they steal from the government or harass the citizen.

In addition to the proceeds from the sole duty of 6 percent on imports and exports, the king of Spain allocates to the province of Louisiana, for the total expenses of its administration, a sum of 650,000 piastres gourdes, including funds for the army and navy.[33] This amount, used with the good management, talents, and honesty of a governor who would indeed occupy himself with the prosperity of the colony, would long ago have presented some very considerable advantages and hastened the time when the grateful colony would have ceased to be a burden to the royal treasury, and would have covered its own expenses by collecting duties on its consumer goods and commodities. But it has always been quite different. The heads of the government and their assistants have squandered the colony's funds. One of them destroyed confidence in the paper money which he gave in payment of his obligations, and which he acquired with his own silver and sometimes even that of the king.[34] Another has made some deals in which the contracting party gave back a large part of the agreed price; and, finally, all excelled only in the thousand and one ways of emptying the public treasury in order that, the use of the local paper money making it seem legal, the possible savings passed with impunity to their own profit.[35]

In the customhouse it is even worse; there the employees, dependent on and absolute strangers to the workings of the intendant's office, were supposed to pay into the treasury the total amount of the duties collected. However, as annoyed as they are aware of the value of the cake that they are not sharing, they know, as cautious individuals, how at least to take their own slice, while not even leaving to the one with whom they are dealing the need to bribe them. Individually and to the detriment of each other, or together, they dream up ways of depriving the treasury of part or all of what is due it. And by common consent, in agreement with the importer of *pacotilles* or cargoes, they grade as mediocre or damaged that which is of extra quality or undamaged; and they alter the weights to their own advantage and appropriate a fourth of the duties legitimately owed, while cutting them in half.[36] The office of the intendant, which clothes itself with all the appearance of conforming to the regulations, opposes these arrangements as well as it can; arrangements which at the same time also diminish the part that falls to its lot in handling; but it is in vain. Pillage covers itself with another cloak in spite of what the intendant's office tries to do, and woe unto him who would not buy the right to cheat the sovereign! A strict enforcement of the entry procedure would then bring delay or harm to his business.

This is how the finances of the province are administered, and it is one of the truths about which I have less fear of contradiction, for in my capacity as a merchant it was necessary for me to yield again and again to the flood of fiscal depravity. I shall not estimate to what extent the customs receipts have increased each year, since in my summary of commerce, as well as agriculture, it will be easy to determine what they should have produced. Moreover, from what I have just said about finances, one would have an incorrect basis for calculations in using their statistics regarding the resources of the country. Be that as it may, I shall admit that some savings have escaped pillage. But alas! It is only for a moment, and how, with past experience, can one expect that in future these savings will be judiciously and equitably employed to the best advantage of the province?

It would be reasonable to suppose that, in a province whose mother country makes good the administrative expenses without any reciprocal business to provide compensation, the head of finances would convince himself of the direct profit in his favor if he furthered all the means of imports in order to encourage the planter who, his needs being adequately

23

supplied, would tend by his labors to increase the fees that enlarge the revenue in the treasury under the intendant's control. This action could not have any political inconvenience, unless it be considered that of binding the population more securely to the sovereign through the advantage of free trade which no other government could perhaps provide them. And, in addition, by the guarantee of an outlet for its commodities which, because of Spain's scorn or indifference, would otherwise rot in the planter's possession. Nevertheless, it would be a mistake to imagine this happening in the province of Louisiana. Convincing proofs of this statement will be given in the section of my observations and notes on commerce and agriculture, and a recent example supports what I shall have to say in that regard. The commodities which the New Orleans market provides for export having now opened up an extensive reciprocal business for it, a ship of the United States arrived from Jamaica, bringing a quantity of silver along with several other articles, all of which were the result of business transactions which had caused it to put into port. It is difficult to believe, but the intendant decided that this silver, brought into port to purchase commodities from the colony, should pay duty along with the rest of the cargo. Thus, as he was driving away hard money, the arrival of which seemed to predict happiness and wealth for the colony, it was necessary, in order to avoid the intendant's inept persecution, to enter this silver as foreign property. Except for that, it would not have been used to purchase commodities in the colony, but this merchant who in good faith did not want to resort to a subterfuge, has acquired by that step the right to export to the United States, and without paying duties, the same amount of specie. Such is the way the intendant's office knows how to provide obstructions even in the case of minor transactions. A trifle that in all other countries would seem unworthy of the attention of an ordinary customs man occupies the time of the chief administrator, not a matter of hours, but entire days, and causes the authorities to be needlessly despised when they would have so many means of being cultivated.

What I have just described regarding the two principal branches of the colony's administration should help to explain what I intend to say regarding their moral and political influence. One has the treasury in its grasp, and the other wields the bayonet, and both nearly always have an attitude of rage and envy. The quarrels between the two principal leaders of the colony have often increased the difficulties that caused its lethargy. Because she wanted to balance the powers of one against the other, Spain has given them a thousand ways of opposing each other, and in the general administration, as in finances, the best intentions for the prosperity of the country were nullified if the vices or incapacity of one of the leaders created obstacles to their fulfillment.

CHAPTER TWO

Police, Judiciary, Population, Customs, and Religion

The governor general is the active head of the police and
courts of justice for the maintenance of good order; and, for
the defense of the province, he has first a regiment of two
battalions known as the Louisiana Regiment, part of which is
scattered throughout the settlements. Then a battalion that
the viceroy of Mexico furnishes to complement the garrison
at New Orleans, several cavalrymen serving almost exclusively in the mail service and the mounted police, and some
artillerymen—in fact, all too few in numbers to form an army
corps without some of the militia joining the regulars. The
governor general presides over the municipal council, called
cabildo in Spanish, consisting of aldermen, judges, an attorney general, and clerks. He appoints the military and civil
commander in each district who, unlike the governor, has no
advisor or more properly a consulting attorney. This official
then becomes in actual fact, acccording to law, recorder or
inexpert judge of civil court cases, and assumes a dual character from the moment he is named to his post, for the
intendant also appoints him as his deputy, and the sword in
that case submits to the pen. The governor arranges to have

appointed, or he himself appoints, police deputies in the various districts, and, in reserving ultimately for himself the immediate control of all police, does not share the glory with anyone if the result is satisfactory, but carries in good spirit all the blame if it is bad.

The law courts have some exceptions to the general rules of procedure, the particulars of which I shall not go into because one would have to be a Spaniard to understand the motives. The intendancy has its private court and assessor in certain cases; some individuals are not subject to the general laws of the population; and I do not speak only of the tribunal before which the civil and criminal cases are usually brought, a court for which the governor general signs the judgments, except for appeal or confirmation from Cuba.

Let us see, first of all, whether the manner in which the police have been supervised has contributed to the security and growth of the colony. As the governor general personally directs the police in New Orleans and its suburbs, his conduct serves as a model for his subordinate officers entrusted with police supervision in the various districts. His direction in reality restricts, just as his casualness relaxes and his arrogance discourages, as, in fact, the abuses of his authority intimidate or disgust. The city of New Orleans, in order to maintain its security, good order, and healthfulness, requires daily supervision for which the governor should rely on others. These include drainage of the city, street cleaning, reliability of its patrols, surveillance of gambling houses, inspection of dance halls and theatres, and immediate imprisonment of vagrants and fugitive slaves. And there are many other minute supervisory details which the governor places under his own immediate jurisdiction, which ought to be delegated to the subordinates with whom the law surrounds him, and by whom he should make it a duty to have their authority respected. The commanders and deputies of the rural districts ought to be encouraged and upheld in the

27

orders and supervision which as masters they would demand: such as in control of slaves; upkeep of roads, levees, and bridges; and the allotment of road gangs as required by law. It is within the municipal council, in the audiences which he would give to his headquarters staff and subordinate police officers, and by communicating with the commanders and deputies in the remote districts, that the governor ought to obtain the stimulus for reform or innovation. It is by tactful supervision administered soundly, so necessary in a superior officer, that he ought to assure himself of faithfulness in relations with his deputies. It is, finally, in the moral and physical aspect of the colony entrusted to him that he should seek the evidence of his good or bad administration. Good order then established on a firm basis, a governor would not be deprived of the time he should devote to the political relationships of a province, and he could concern himself with plans for incentives or improvements which the mother countries owe to their colonies when they want to hold on to them.

Why then have the governor generals of Louisiana generally not adopted this procedure, since the means to do so are offered to them by law, and by the extent of the authority vested in them? Because that would be to deny themselves the many opportunities to increase the salaries which the king pays; and permitting the apparent authority of the minor officials to be degraded, they satisfy their own interests even more than their vanity. From that tainted source flows all the corruption in the police of New Orleans. *Regidores* or municipal officers are useless; an attorney general would try in vain to enforce the claims of citizens; *alcaldes* or justices of the peace are powerless to do good. The office of ward commissioner that Carondelet created and honored has fallen into disrepute.[1] The patrols are insignificant; the garrison is inconsequential; the militia not in uniform; and the slightest remedy for all these disorders is always

28

exclusively in the hands of the person who causes them.

In reading my *Observations*, it will be difficult to understand how I could be justified in blaming with so much bitterness all those involved in administration; and only an eyewitness can be convinced of such truth. Indeed, it must have been seen in order to describe to what extremes they have carried the laxity and neglect of the police. The patrols in town are so poorly organized that nighttime burglaries in the warehouses are frequent, as are murders among the vagrants. Despite engineers whom they have repeatedly employed to survey the land, and convicts to make the necessary embankments and excavations, there is stagnant and putrid water in many streets, and the drainage canals are clogged. Hundreds of licensed taverns openly sell to slaves, and, in making them drunk, become throughout the day and night receivers of goods stolen from their masters. And those gambling houses are openly protected where the swindler and adventurer rob the inexperienced young man as well as the father of a family who is forgetful of his duties. A public ball, where those who have a bit of discretion prefer not to appear, organized by the free people of color, is each week the gathering place for the scum of such people and of those slaves who, eluding their owner's surveillance, go there to bring their plunder. There is a gambling table at the ball where the happiest rascal appropriates for himself what others have stolen; and as a crowning infamy one finds even some white people who repeatedly battle with the slaves for places in the quadrilles, and for their share of the household pilferage which they decide by a throw of the dice. The government is aware of and permits all of that; and woe unto the minor official who would want to stop it. The governor general reserves to himself alone the right to decide when gambling causes abuses, and whether the unproductivity of such activities would affect the public well-being.

The out-lying districts are not treated any better; the same laxity abounds there. Negroes, less subject to authority and more able to move around without supervision on the main roads and in town, are in a position to learn the ways of a corruption which they impart to one another by degrees; and the anxious owner lives in a state of war with his slaves at a time when paternal attentions of the government could enable him to use them profitably. The roads have deep holes; the levees and bridges are not maintained; and every time the Mississippi rises substantially, it causes crevasses that obstruct the roads and ruin the planters, leaving putrid remains of fish, snakes, and animals on the land after the waters have receded, the emanations of which, mingling with the noxious stench of the filthy city, cause periodic fevers that decimate the foreigner and bring desolation to the families of the colonists.

The navigation of streams, which the silt from water of a flat and muddy land hinders daily, is no longer a matter of concern to the government. A canal that Carondelet had opened to provide a more convenient, safer, and less costly access to the lakes north of New Orleans and to West Florida, deteriorates from day to day; and its course, like the mouth of the little stream with which it connects, is filling up so rapidly that soon pirogues will hardly be able to enter it.[2] The mouth of the Mississippi, which the huge mass of its waters changes or obstructs at will, has not yet had any of the government's attention to improve or maintain it. Many times in the course of a year the negligence, laziness, or ignorance of the river pilots endanger the life or fortune of the traveler. Perhaps Spain, finally, will know what she ought to have done for the happiness and prosperity of this colony only after her lack of concern and the mistakes of her administration will have caused her to lose it.

If such is the maintenance of good order in the province of Louisiana, what are its courts of justice like? I shall not permit myself to enter into any details in their regard; nor shall I go into the constant deviations of their trickery and corruptness to seek, among the multitude of examples, some of the more striking ones. May the widows and orphans dry their tears; may the honest citizens persist in fleeing from the need to have recourse to the courts of justice; and may the judges, or the elected justices of the peace, increase through their good offices the means of amicably ending disputes among citizens, when such disputes are not outside of the often precarious authority with which the courts are invested.

The population of Louisiana, Spanish by its government, is still generally French in its tastes, customs, habits, religion, and language. Gay, noisy, hospitable, and easy to govern, it would need more education to moderate its passions, and especially to curb the fickleness, curiosity, and sometimes envy that so often trouble the welfare of its community life, stifling in the heart of the foreigner the sentiment of gratitude which the population's original graciousness had inspired. The physical traits are generally handsome, especially among the women. The Creole is born with the happiest of dispositions; the companionship among those who have visited Europe is gentle and trustworthy; but for the others in general, politeness is only the glow of an innate gift which careful upbringing has not helped arm against that kind of emotionalism which, for better or worse, ignorance provokes and which malicious persons know so well how to turn to their advantage. The Creoles love pleasure and dissipation; the male is tireless in hunting; and both sexes throughout the colony have a particular passion for dancing. In the countryside they give themselves over to this exercise so long as work in the fields allows it; and in town, anticipation of the balls compensates during nine months for many social privations, as their enjoyment during the winter months leaves nothing to be desired for the happiness of those whose frugality or wealth results in their making a brilliant appearance at the balls. This fondness for the dance is not only indulged in from adolescence to old age, the youngest children also have their balls where the parent's infatuation brings them each week into a show of luxury and affectation. And this establishment, authorized by the government, is perhaps unique in the world, as it is immoral in the eyes of every intelligent and thinking man. The arts are hardly cultivated at all, because the situation of the colony up to this day has not prospered enough to attract teachers and have them settle there. The customs were often cited for their simplicity; and throughout the colony there was a good-naturedness and confidence which frequent exposure to strangers began to change, and which luxury will soon succeed in eliminating unless the wealth of the colony does not continue the progress that it has made.

The population of Louisiana consists now, in Spanish subjects, of about 30,000 whites and 25,000 blacks or mulattoes, concerning which it has been impossible for me to secure an accurate census. It started to develop in the same general manner as all the other colonies. Some Frenchmen, Germans, and Canadians came at different times to settle here, and Spaniards in turn became part of the population through their government. Because they were so near, some Englishmen moved to Louisiana; and many citizens of the western settlements of the United States finally established their residence, resulting, particularly in New Orleans, in an assortment of manners, customs, languages, and interests which must have caused the change in the habits and that egotistical attitude unique to the original settlers.

Religion is perhaps the segment of the colony's administration over which Spain has had the least influence. It is claimed that at one time she intended to establish a tribunal of the Inquisition, but the colonial government was successfully able to make the court at Madrid realize the danger of such a course, and the priests, to their chagrin, were not able to defile the province with this monstrous establishment. They are, nevertheless, not without some authority, and woe unto the man who, not piously kissing their hand, falls under their control! Then they are all the more severe, since they have few occasions to exercise their authority. Fanaticism, pride, and partiality guide all of their activities; and I have seen a very respectable friend slandered by them in a most atrocious manner and brought before their court, because he had been married in a remote post, as was done since the colony's establishment. As a result, he was obliged to undergo an annoying procedure, similar in all respects to the inquisitorial iniquity. I learned that, fortunately, His Grace, the Bishop, had invoked some leniency. Even more fortunate, however, the means which the priests have of victimizing people are few indeed; and, reduced to annoying several hypocrites of their own nation, while quarreling among themselves in their sacristies, they do not have the power to meddle in the conduct of citizens, but are obliged to allow religion to remain in the relaxed state that it was throughout the French colonies. The clergy refuse, nevertheless, to bury in consecrated ground those who have not fulfilled their Christian duties before dying, and this is their final outburst of fanaticism on a prey that they could not seize while alive.

CHAPTER THREE

Commerce

First of all I am going to give some views on commerce in order to show to what extent its existence must have been precarious, and how justified it would be to blame the Spanish government which has probably always been convinced that in Louisiana it was only necessary to pay some military officers and a regiment in order to keep it in subjection, and to hire some financiers to monopolize its trade. I shall not go into the details of the colony's commercial situation before the Spaniards took possession. I should in that case have had to place much blame on several French administrators, who, monopolists or speculators, working for their own private account and not for the advancement and prosperity of the colony, caused the government to lose interest in it.[1] Nevertheless, at the time of the peace that preceded the cession of Louisiana to Spain, [Jean Jacques] d'Abbadie, who was named intendant and governor, occupied himself mainly with efforts to enable the colony to flourish, either by hampering speculation and monopoly, or in holding down expenses and facilitating the export of commodities or, finally, in opening up commerce to the

British.[2] The colony already saw its wealth increasing. D'Abbadie's successor had not, as a matter of fact, developed the same administrative talents.[3] But whatever may have been the condition of commerce then, the bloody taking possession of Louisiana by O'Reilly, its first [second] Spanish governor, plunged the colony into misery and mourning. And I intend to lay stress only on what its new masters did to bring commerce to the situation in which it now finds itself.

It is well known that the manufactured products of Spain provide almost nothing for the consumer needs of its colonies. Moreover, in spite of all the exclusive privileges granted to commerce by the mother country and nearly always with the concurrence of that host of guards and greedy employees paid to prevent it, contraband trade in peacetime, as in war, provides nearly all the articles of luxury and essential needs for the large and fertile Spanish possessions in the New World and, as a consequence, acquires most of the wealth. This contraband trade, that usually enriches those who engage in it, opens to all civil and military officials the road to a fortune as certain as it is very bright, and becomes of great advantage to the manufactured products of other European nations who are then not at all interested in invading those possessions, and whose profits are actually greater than Spain's.

Louisiana—which Spain surely wanted to possess only so as no longer to see a French colony grow larger at the mouth of a river whose branches lead to the borders of Mexico—has been subjected to an altogether special administration. The mother country, in not deigning to furnish it with supplies, either abandoned it to the necessity of a contraband trade with the English, the occupants of the Mississippi's [left] bank that now belongs to the United States, or, by some more or less hampered privileges, gave it the means of securing its supplies from foreign countries. Spain, who needed tobacco, only occasionally allowed Louisiana to export some to her;

and France, cruelly mercenary regarding that colony when she sold it to Spain, from the time of the American independence until her own revolution continued to import almost exclusively all the products of Louisiana, either in her European ports or by coastwide trade with her colonies. Louisiana was prevented from having any dealings with other Spanish colonies, except to exchange carefully selected goods designated by, and at the whim of, their officials. These included rosin, tar, and lumber. Thus, isolated like a gangrenous growth from the body of the state, but useful for the preservation of one of its members [Mexico], the Louisianians were always Spanish in name, French at heart, and often ran the risk of contraband trade with foreigners.

If, by closing her eyes to the sources of prosperity which the passage of time, in spite of any government, should bring to the mouth of the Mississippi, the intention of Spain by such an administration was to allow a colony to vegetate, which seemed useful to her by its location but dangerous by its population (because it was French), then she could not have adopted a better plan. At the time of my arrival, the indifference in the colony, I could say its hatred for the government, was at a peak. Agriculture was almost nonexistent, and commerce—in fact always concerned regarding its imports and always in the embarrasing situation of having an insignificant amount of goods to exchange with foreign countries—had the sole resource of exporting fraudulently the piastres that the mother country allocates to cover the expenses of the province.[4]

Nevertheless, my interest was aroused by several indications of activity in commerce; and my attention was called to some instances of river trade in the upper reaches of the Mississippi, as much with the settlements along its banks as with those along the streams which flow into it.[5] I considered carefully the advantages that should accrue to New Orleans by the periodic growth of that river trade, but an event aroused my uncertainty and—coupled with the knowledge that I had acquired regarding the actual meager resources of Louisiana—it seemed to confirm my fears that the grandeur of this province would still be hampered for years to come.

This event was the choice which the chamber of commerce deigned to make of me as one of the syndics to represent it before the government. I had not been in the colony a year, and this nomination, which in all respects should have been flattering to me, was nonetheless surprising since I had never attended any of the meetings of the chamber that had selected me to represent it. Be that as it may, at the moment I write this, the syndics of the chamber of commerce in their relations with the Spanish government have generally been no more than passive individuals from whom it asks advice when they might be of assistance, and whose complaints and comments it rejects when contrary to the interests and views of the official to whom they are addressed. And although I must say that during my first four years (1796–1799) in New Orleans there was hardly enough trade to justify a chamber of commerce, yet it is a fact that in the dealings I had with the government at that time, I learned how the prosperity of the colony was hampered. Moreover, I seemed to see clearly then that Louisiana would stagnate in mediocrity as long as the Spanish court would not employ other means to govern it and to make it prosper, and that Spain would not realize how important this colony could become among her remaining American possessions.

If I saw the military arm of the government always more readily inclined to favor commerce and business establishments, I also saw quite often the fiscal authorities, on whom commerce more immediately depends, impede its most urgent transactions, either for supplying the colony or exporting its commodities. And that situation—either through mistaken need for severity or by personal interest—was

37

always covered over by the cloak of obedience to the laws. I saw more: the humiliation and discouragement in which a Spanish customs officer can hold the commerce of a country; the excessive covetousness of the employees when the ambiguity of their regulations puts you, to some extent, at their mercy; and, their annoying pettiness when you place them in the position of not being able to get anything out of you. Finally, I saw how—lacking prudence and understanding, and with no advantage to the government—the total amount of taxes and the 500,000 to 600,000 piastres that the king of Spain sends every year for the maintenance of this colony, goes to pay the beneficiaries of a thieving treasury, indifferent to the welfare of the country and to the mistakes of the government's irresolute system. Those are the additional reasons which seemed to me should retard the success of the province of Louisiana; and in that connection I have already presented a comprehensive view in my preceding observations on administrative affairs.

The more I acquired knowledge about conditions in the colony, the less I thought I should congratulate myself on the position to which I had been appointed, because of the difficulty I perceived in being able to do anything useful for my associates under an administration rather inclined to controversy than stability. The more I reflected on the present condition of commerce, the more I acquired information about the past; and, finally, the more I concerned myself with the future, greater again was my perplexity. What! During thirty years, I said to myself, that the Spaniards have owned this vast and fertile colony they have paid fifteen to twenty million piastres for the expenses of the government, and yet as my investigations show, there has not been any growth! A few businessmen in comfortable circumstances, equal in number to those who had preceded them, barely achieved success, and the planter became poorer and worn-out in fruitless labors. The treasury interfered constantly and

Introduction

Si les Circonstances me mettent dans le Cas de livrer à l'Impression mes observations sur la Louysiane, je m'attends qu'elles trouveront beaucoup de Contradicteurs, surtout parmi ceux qui trompés par les détails qu'ils ont vu sur cette partie du Nouveau monde, n'y ont trouvé en venant la visiter qu'ennui, pertes & malheurs; qui nous vu en se rendant par les derrières des Etats unis que les Rives souvent inhabitées de l'Ohio, et les bords plats & fangeux du mississipi; qui rendus à la nouvelle-Orléans, n'ont voulu y voir pendant leur séjour que des moyens présents, sans chercher à approfondir les véritables Causes de sa médiocrité; et qui enfin se sont épouvantés de l'Insalubrité d'un sol dont l'insouciance & la negligence du Gouvernement empoisonnent & perpétuent les Inconvénients.

Je ne me dissimule point que ces observations portent avec elles un Caractère d'Imperfection, pour lequel je n'aurais pas le droit de réclamer de l'Indulgence, si je me piquais d'être littérateur; mais entrainé par le genre de mes occupations loin des études qui le forment, je les offrirai telles qu'elles se trouvent rédigées. J'aurais voulu en dieu de parler avec autant de détails des torts de l'administration, mais j'ai cru ne pouvoir m'en dispenser. Je devais répondre à l'objection qui m'a été souvent faite contre la Louysiane, en me citant que la france ne l'avait cédée que parce qu'elle avait reconnu l'Improfitabilité d'en tirer parti, et que l'on des Espagnols n'avait pu depuis trente ans la tirer de la misère. La Louysiane a plus qu'aucune autre Colonie seule Combien un Gouvernement pouvait en entraver les ressources, et bientot elle prouvera que les avantages réunis de Sa Situation pouvoient en surmonter la plus maligne influence. Ce motif m'a particulièrement engagé à entrer dans des détails qui pourront quelquefois paraître minutieux, mais qui multipliés à l'Infini dans la marche du Gouvernement n'en ont pas moins occasionné cette stagnation de médiocrité qui faisait politiquement mépriser la possession de la Louysiane.

Je n'entreprends point ces observations pour la publicité, mais sur les bruits de la Retrocession de la Louysiane à la france, je me réservai d'en faire l'hommage au Ministère de sa metropole, si vraiment elle était retrocédée, ou au moins de les Communiquer aux negociants qui pourraient s'occuper des plus se Commerce que je leur offrirai. J'ai fait tout ce qui a dépendu de moi pour savoir la vérité. J'ai gardé le Silence sur les choses dont je n'ai pas au moins obtenu la Certitude morale, et si par hazard ma Critique du Gouvernement paraissait d'une personnalité outrée, je ne puis me référer qu'à l'approbation qu'en donnerait, je crois, tout homme impartial domicilié ou Voyageur. Quoiqu'il en soit, que l'on n'aille pas me Confondre avec les précheurs d'Insurrection auxquels je rougirais d'être assimilé. Les torts du Gouvernement Espagnol à la Louysiane sont de ceux qui perpétuent la médiocrité d'un pays, mais

Map of the Mississippi and Its Branches, attributed to Barthélemy Lafon,

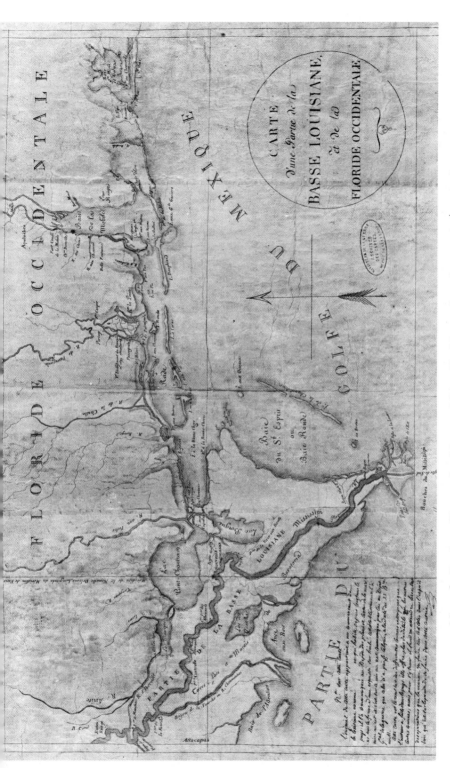

Map of a Portion of Lower Louisiana and West Florida, attributed to Barthélemy Lafon,
from Service Historique de l'Armée, Section Moderne, Vincennes

Courtesy of Photographie Giraudon, Paris

Residence of James Pitot in New Orleans, *ca.* 1800–1802,
from watercolor by Boyd Cruise

Courtesy of Mrs. J. St. Clair Favrot

Pitot House on Bayou St. John, 1979 photograph by Jean Jeffers;
currently owned and operated by the Louisiana Landmarks Society

Pitot House on Bayou St. John, sketch *ca.* 1830 by Charles-Alexandre LeSueur

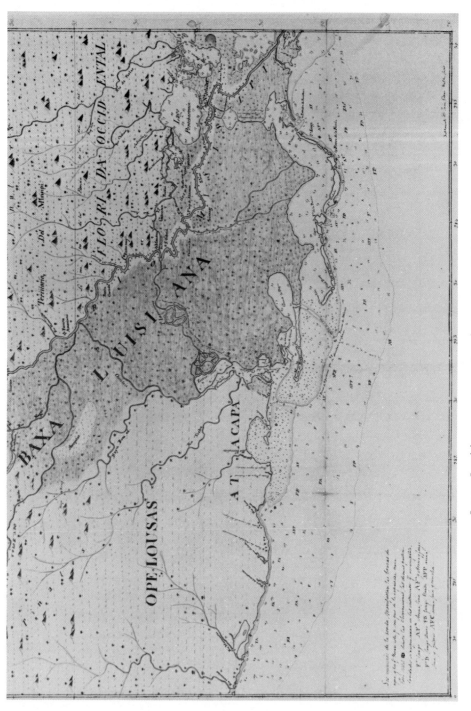

Lower Louisiana, *ca.* 1799–1803, by Don Juan Pedro Walke

devised new monopolies; and the military government—rightly disturbed in the past about the maneuvers of the French representatives to the United States, but perhaps in error as to the inhabitants of Louisiana in general—found it difficult not to see again, in the mass of the population, the group of revolutionaries whom they had suspected when France and Spain were at war.

Confidence was not yet reestablished. The hatreds between Spaniards and Frenchmen were not at an end; and even though some unexpected successes had strengthened the alliance between the two powers, one could foresee the inevitability of disturbances and misfortunes concerning which one had only been apprehensive. On what then, after all, could I base my hopes, since the local merchant's discouragement was at its peak? The businessman, whose cargo in a ship under the United States flag had escaped by a miracle in coming here, was rarely adventurous enough to gamble that his ship in returning to its home port would not be overtaken by English privateers who, before the war with Spain, would recognize it only as of French ownership, and after the declaration of war, wanted to seize all United States ships as being of Spanish ownership.[6] In either event the ship was taken to Bermuda or New Providence [in British West Indies], harbors that exist to the shame of humanity only by an odious piracy and where losses by pillage or condemnation were twice what they would have been if the ship had been convoyed coming here. After all, could I then expect more growth for this colony in times of war and revolution? No. But fortunately some compelling circumstances, almost totally unexpected, suddenly gave it the pleasant aspect of approaching happiness; and from the distant places where navigation on the Mississippi can penetrate, as from the territory near the mouth of this river, Louisiana acquired riches which were much more certain guarantors of its prosperity than the piastres it received from Mexico; and in giving to commerce the support and trade for business ventures, did more in four years than had been done in thirty years of Spanish adminsitration.

I shall confine myself, with regard to commerce before my arrival in the colony, to the particulars that I have just given and I am now going to trace briefly the administration's conduct with respect to commerce during the five years that have preceded all of my observations. It is the only aspect that I shall refer to regarding a commerce lacking foundation, sustenance, and stability. Eyewitness for several years to its languishing beginnings, I shall give an idea of the hindrances it had to endure in the decisions gratuitously made by the government, contrary to those that might have been able to help it; and the details that I shall give, in backing them up with several explanatory notes, will justify the harsh severity with which I shall continue to speak. But God forbid that I be accused of wanting to insult the Spanish character. It is their colonial government in general that I undertake to censure; and it is particularly the one of Louisiana that I wish to unmask, as much in the execution, so crooked and arbitrary, of orders from Madrid, as in the distrust and politics that result in cutting off the population of this province from commercial dealings with other Spanish possessions. I should like to prove that this prohibition—which they consider as a favor in that it opens direct commerce with foreign countries to this colony by preference—became, as a result of the chains with which politics and the abuse of power hampered Louisiana, the cause of stagnation in its resources during the period that preceded the kind of trade explosion [with Americans] by which Louisianians have made themselves known.

Baron de Carondelet, a Frenchman by birth, who governed at the time of my arrival—and in which capacity he missed being a source of happiness for this colony only by his having reached it during the period when the French Revolution recalled memories of their former homeland to its inhabitants—held both the intendancy and military government for some time. Whether he had been misled by treacherous spies or circumstances which had made him take severe measures, in all fairness one should at least admit that, as long as he was intendant and governor, he favored commerce as something that should bring prosperity to the colony. Not only did he promote contacts with the outside world, in acting on his own before receiving the court's authorization and for the welfare of the colony by opening shipping with the United States, but he also used all his authority, even when he no longer acted as intendant, to obtain a tariff for commerce which, by the exact assessment of duties and their reduction to 6 percent, saved the colony as much as he could from the shameful slavery in which custom officials held it.[7] One might say that Carondelet had found only peddlers in New Orleans, and that he wanted to establish businessmen there. He also took several steps in favor of agriculture and wished to do even more, but the court had reestablished the former division of authority which exists today, and commerce again took on the chains that Carondelet's good intentions had only been able to reduce in weight. In judging impartially the conduct of that administrator, one would deplore the political circumstances which kept him from improving the condition of the colony. If he was quite pleased when the Franco-Spanish alliance [1796] had banished all fears of local insurrection or conquest from abroad, then is when he would have been free to initiate his helpful ideas. Furthermore, if no longer seeing in each inhabitant an enemy of his sovereign or his authority, Carondelet had governed completely differently from the unyielding methods of the other officials, then instead of hostility toward him by some of the population, the entire colony would have regretted to see him leave and would have wished him well, because he had hastened its prosperity and had convinced Louisiana of its importance.

41

Gayoso succeeded Carondelet, and I was still one of the syndics of commerce when he became governor. In the service of the colony for a long time, he was commandant at Natchez when the United States, by virtue of their treaty [Pinckney Treaty of 1795], came in the spring of the same year to take over that place and establish their boundaries. Carondelet avoided it as long as he held the reins of government, but Gayoso thought or felt constrained to act differently and handed over Natchez [1799] and named some commissioners to trace the boundaries which separate the territory of the United States from Lower Louisiana and the Floridas.[8] This event caused me to jot down some observations which I entitled *Memoir to Communicate to the Commercial Interests of New Orleans*, and which I presented to several businessmen who praised my views. But, aside from them, I met only the aloofness and indifference which come from being accustomed to restraints, instead of the enthusiasm which united free and active men for their benefit and the welfare of their fellow citizens. Governor Gayoso heard comments about that memoir and asked me for a copy, and in expressing his profuse thanks even assured me that he would send it to the court, adding to it some observations which had not yet occurred to me in view of the short time that I had been in the colony, but which supported what I had written. Did he send it? I do not know, but what is certain is that since then only one *cédula* or royal order has arrived from the court, about whichI shall have occasion to speak later, which resulted in the ruin of the colony during the remainder of the war [1796–1801]; and if New Orleans has taken several more steps towards her future grandeur, it is only through the effect of her fortunate position on the American continent.

That memoir, which was only a short analysis hastily put together on subjects that I undertake to deal with today, will provide me with some observations to insert here. At the time I wrote it, I was familiar with the regions to which the mouth of the Mississippi offers the unique outlet for their commerce, having examined them on a map. Since then, a long and difficult voyage has changed my theory into practice in that respect, and I shall venture today to guarantee results which at that time I offered only as encouragements.

The [Pinckney] treaty that Spain had just made with the United States not only gave them ownership of the left bank of the Mississippi, beginning just beyond Natchez, but also gave them the right of free navigation in all that portion of Lower Louisiana where both sides belong to Spain. Spain also undertook to furnish to the United States a place of deposit at New Orleans for the supplies of their upper territories, while preventing them from making any sales in the New Orleans market. Without going deeply at this moment into all the reasons which should have kept the Spanish court from ever having given up the left bank of the Mississippi to the United States, I confine myself to the consequences of the exclusion from the New Orleans market. It was that Spain—who never concerned herself with nor supplied the colony, neither did she buy its products—wanted to limit cargoes during wartime to her own ships; an exclusion that has surely given the appearance of favoring local commerce, but that in reality carried with it the coup de grâce for the colony up to the moment when some power, through pity, would have deigned to conquer it.

I noted in my memoir that if they had required without exception that cargoes destined to go up the Mississippi River in ships of the United States could only be warehoused, then the commerce of New Orleans would have found itself reduced to practically nothing, and businessmen would have been obliged to take their capital and abilities elsewhere, since the rate of duty on foreign shipments had prevented them from making any sales at New Orleans. The American flag would have flown on all ships loaded with cargoes for the Spanish possessions as well as for the United States. Some would have stored goods with commission houses, or those firms with which they were associated, for transshipment up the river as far as the most distant ports. Others, under the protection of their country's flag, would have stayed longer in the river; there they would have resorted to smuggling in exchanging their cargoes for commodities of Louisiana, as well as those of any other place beyond its boundaries. Finally, smugglers as well as warehousemen would have brazenly carried off, right in front of the port of New Orleans, all available profits on the supplies and products of the countries which communicate by navigation on one of the finest rivers in the world. The city merchant and the country person, braving the hazards of smuggling, one with his money the other with his farm products, would have sought either an assortment of goods or necessary supplies. The planter or businessman from far-distant communities, coming down the river with richly laden boats, would have traded with the ships on their route which they might have met near New Orleans. Their goods having been left with them, and agreeing to finish trading later, they would come into port perhaps to dispose of their cargo's shoddy remnants and either replenish supplies or wind up their affairs. In fact, if some commerce was still carried on, it would have only been clandestine, and in that case the attractions of profit on one side and the severity of fiscal laws on the other, would have created a kind of commerce that is always contrary to the precepts of a wise and beneficial government.

Under those circumstances, who would then have been able to benefit? Would it be the Spanish government, obliging gatekeeper of the Mississippi, which had surrounded itself with a regiment of extortioners, not even collecting enough duties for their wages, and which had abrogated its rights to the colonists' obedience and affection? Would it be the planter or businessman located in the Spanish settlements? If they had thought so, their mistaken opinion could have been easily disproved. By preventing foreigners from depriving New Orleans of the rich market that its location promises, would it not benefit the planter or businessman to be able to buy at better prices? Would that not also be true even though, at the same price among the variety of supplies which a buyer acquired through fraudulent and unprofitable trading, or which a seller received clandestinely for his exchangable goods? Who then, in fact, might have gained there? Only the United States, as I shall have the occasion to prove later on.

I do not know whether it would be too damaging to say that the government had poorly informed the court before the treaty [of 1795], or if a compelling reason had led it to this important and dangerous cession [of the Natchez district] which even in times of peace will, for a long period, continue to keep the government holding both sides of the Mississippi River in a kind of state of war. Carondelet realized that the effect [of Pinckney's Treaty] was going to be as unexpected for New Orleans as it was ruinous, and took several steps to remedy it. He agreed that all American ships could put their cargoes up for sale in New Orleans, and would be subject only to the payment of the same duties as those owned by Spain. Before that decision was made ships coming from abroad, being hampered in a most ridiculous manner by permits which were required in order to enter the Mississippi, found that at least they had to have influence to obtain from the intendant the signal favor of seeing that the colony, which the king confined to his care in that regard, did not want for those things most necessary to its existence. The English knew about these intrigues and, with that as a pretext, harassed the ships of the United States destined for New Orleans. The local merchant who still carried on business for his own account was compelled to assume all the risks himself, in order to supply a country of which he was a creditor, and on whose destiny his entire fortune depended. And the foreigner who speculated in imports there for his own account, under the umbrella of special arrangements, was always the dupe either of his confidence in the reports being made to him, or of the calculation on which he had based the expectation of a profit.

This modification of the treaty [1798], by facilitating and assuring future business transactions on the part of the government, was an indispensible measure for the colony. But it was not extended as far as it should have been for its own advantage, and, I would venture to say, for the colony's survival. For, as I had already indicated in my memoir, and as commerce continually demanded, it would have been necessary to permit entry into the port of New Orleans, as reason and politics dictated, not only American ships but indeed all foreign ships that would have wanted to come to enrich their commerce.

The government, which neither provided nor protected, was on the verge of plunging New Orleans again into the situation [warehousing and contraband trade] for which the treaty provided. Fortunately, the objections of the business community were heeded when the intendant revealed his proposals, and he did not demand, as he had planned, that ships destined from New Orleans to the settlements in the United States, our providers and suppliers at the time, pay an export duty of 6 percent on their cargoes. That would again have necessitated the warehousing of goods and a contraband trade, since they would never agree under those circumstances to have American ships ascend the river as far as the limits of their possessions. That requirement was indeed opposed to the views that I expressed on the subject of duties, regarding which I asked for a reduction, considering that the 6 percent import and export duties were too high not to give rise to contraband trade, especially in exports. The outcome has already justified my estimates many times. When regulations harass, businessmen force themselves, in order to lighten their burden, to come to terms with those very same persons in charge of collecting duties. And in the reduction of the duty I did not have in mind only the decrease in the commerce of the country; I also saw there the advantage to the treasury in no longer giving support to the smugglers and in destroying that degrading dealing of businessmen with the hirelings who levy the extortionate duty.

I made one observation about the nature of the duty at New Orleans in case the court would realize the necessity of reducing it. That was that the duty was not levied in the humiliating manner generally assumed in Spanish custom-houses. And that a declaration and oath should not be required from an individual, whose honesty is thereby re-vived by his self-respect and made more important in his own eyes. A ship's cargo or *pacotille* was admitted without forcing a complete unpacking which, by deteriorating the merchan-dise, would annoy both the foreigner and colonist, and would remind them of the advantages of warehousing or contra-band trade rather than expose them to shrinkage of their cargoes often destined for transhipment to settlements upriver.

Another quite interesting matter to request of the court, and already, they had told me, placed several times before His Catholic Majesty, would have been the free exportation of silver. The condition of the province with respect to specie was proof that the severity of the fiscal laws did not prevent its withdrawal from circulation; and the indulgence with which they have sometimes thought they should treat offenders, is proof of the tacit consent of local officials and the court on the necessity of permitting such action. This prohibition against taking silver out of the colony is advantageous only to the guardians of the customhouse who must be bribed, and to whom one pays the duty that would have gone into the royal treasury. How can Spain continue to prevent the export of specie from a country where commerce and agriculture are not sufficiently encouraged so that one can provide commodities in commerce for the supplies that the other furnishes?

I also took the liberty of referring to the exclusion of New Orleans from commerce with Vera Cruz, which is the storehouse of the wealth as well as of the supplies of Mexico; an exclusion even more unjust and ridiculous in time of war, in that it only encourages an odious and reprehensible contraband trade with the enemy. And, the court, hardly providing any escort for its treasure ships and not furnishing any convoy to commercial shipping, opened Vera Cruz a short time later to American vessels.[9] That was to enrich foreigners rather than its own subjects in Lower Louisiana, who can ship there only by the particular favor of their intendant, or by contraband trade at the peril of their freedom and wealth. Nevertheless, since the commerce of Spain can do nothing for her colonies in time of war, New Orleans could become with much less danger and more justice the storehouse where Mexicans, often lacking everything except silver, would purchase their supplies. That privilege, benefiting the government a hundredfold, would once again earn the gratitude and fidelity of the inhabitants of Louisiana. And the government cannot do other than grant such a privilege, since it should do more at all times for the colonists than for neighbors who own the largest part of one of the banks of the Mississippi.

All of these observations were without results, and I ended my memoir by repeating the earnest wishes that Baron de Carondelet, about whom I've often spoken, had expressed for the well-being of commerce, and who wanted to obtain for the business community a position of respectability in which all good government ought to strive to place it. Knowing well that for commercial prosperity the dilatory tactics of lower courts cannot be tolerated, which always make a country's progress uncertain by exciting distrust and creating impediments to its influence, Carondelet had urged that Madrid be asked to establish a consular court. Such a court acts as a restraint on the dishonest man in settling his contracts and ignominiously strikes from the roster of businessmen those whom honor and probity should not have included there. I called upon my fellow citizens to repeat their demands in that regard by telling the local officials, in order to bring them around to supporting it, that without this useful institution, each member of the business community finding himself isolated, his views of special interest to other businessmen would always be unproductive, while those that are useful and beneficial to the public, which they have a right to expect from a group of wealthy men favored by the government, would come to naught. I had often spoken in vain; it was in vain that I wrote. I only learned in how many ways the prosperity of the colony had been retarded before I arrived, and to what extent my fellow citizens had acquired the habit of scheming in the midst of a monopoly system's impediments that had even taken away from them the steadfastness necessary to claim either justice or favors from the sovereign.

A thousand circumstances, too long to retell, convinced me of the uselessness of the syndics of commerce. For instance, there was little inclination on the part of the administration to use them effectively; and the supervision which it exercised prevented the syndics from establishing a fund for themselves, which would have enabled them to create a forceful organization. Thus, I had no other desire than to rid myself of the burden that they had entrusted to me, but I could not bring myself to do this before the journey that I undertook in August, 1798; a journey for which I shall give the motives, and the results of which, as I have already made known, have changed in actual fact the probabilities which I had suspected with regard to Louisiana. If, in going into the details already given and which will follow in the course of my observations on the actual condition of commerce, I have sought to prove

49

that the court of Spain, either by premeditated design or through the ignorance and unfaithfulness of its agents, had generally proceeded in a direction opposite to the prosperity of that colony, it is nonetheless true that by the compelling force of its location Louisiana had already made headway despite the shackles and vices of its administration. The government, however, in a sentiment of apathetic pride allowed the system to remain undistrubed: the policing of the interior was more and more relaxed; the colony was allowed to grow weaker, instead of being supplied and helped to expand; and, failing to have facilitated timely journeys outside the country, commerce could not furnish the planters with the machinery they most urgently needed for the utilization of the sugar mills which they had miraculously established.

I then found myself reduced to a sort of nullity by the combination of all the above circumstances. However, having acquired knowledge of the methods and kinds of materials necessary for a sugar mill, and mainly curious to travel through the countries where there was beginning to form a source of wealth for Lower Louisiana, I undertook an overland journey to the United States, through huge forests to the north of New Orleans. I went by way of Kentucky in order to have manufactured at a newly established ironworks some boilers and sugar mill machinery. The Ohio River, which flows through that state, and the Mississippi—proud to receive into its bosom the waters of a hundred other navigable streams—would surely be able to bring them to their destination, in spite of the enemy's piracy and the lack of concern by the government. My project was successful in many respects, but my business house, as a matter of fact, was cheated in half of the items that I had contracted for it. Many other buyers had the same experience through either negligence or dishonesty in the choice of raw materials by the foundries, but nothing could be blamed on me—the accuracy of the dimensions and designs being perfect. Had the iron foundries been accurate in the execution of my specifications, in their own interest I would have made possible a means of immense wealth for them, which the absence of hostilities and the nearness to markets guaranteed to them by preference. But they have eliminated for a long time all sentiments of confidence in their operations, and one should often expect to be treated thus in newly established countries. Of a hundred men that misfortune or the spirit of enterprise lead there, a thousand of the scum of society pass it by; and with the desire for quick wealth resulting in poor workmanship, they destroy confidence before having achieved it, and among them one finds for a long time more fertility in the soil which they cultivate than morality in their commercial transactions.

I shall not speak at this time about the lands which I had to pass through on my journey, since I plan to reserve a part of my *Observations* not only for the topography of the province of Louisiana, but also for a general and circumstantial view of all the lands whose products will one day enrich the markets of New Orleans, through the necessity of shipping them on the streams that flow into the Mississippi.

I continued my journey as far as Philadelphia by taking into Kentucky the route by which I would pass the headwaters of various large streams which have their source at the center of the United States in the back countries of Virginia and the Carolinas, such as the Cumberland and Tennessee Rivers, and whose navigation is irrevocably dependent on the Mississippi. On my return I came to Fort Pitt to embark with a cargo of goods considered as contraband which the enemy [England] would not allow to pass by sea. I floated down the Ohio which rises out of the convergence of two navigable streams, the Alleghany and the Monongahela, and I saw the mouths of its branches whose courses already irrigate and enrich vast territories on the left bank, and whose headwaters on the right bank, in a volume permitting navigation, often approach very close to the lakes that connect with the St. Lawrence River. Finally, I floated down 300 to 400 leagues on the Mississippi, and I was back in New Orleans on May 18, 1799, after an absence of ten months.

Not having been able, before my departure, to resign my commission as syndic of commerce, I found myself once again so designated upon my return, and my first task was to have myself replaced. Nothing of interest had occurred during my absence, other than an ill-advised order prohibiting ships of the United States from transporting to Havana boards for sugar boxes which, appearing to favor the owners of several Spanish ships, resulted in doubling the losses of the colony. First of all in losing by seizure, for lack of convoy, all the ships which for the rest of the war would probably not be replaced. Then in killing off, until a new order from Madrid, a branch of exports that had made and supported the wealth of many planters. And, finally, in placing the United States in a position to continue and to increase their profitable shipping with the island of Cuba, not only furnishing sugar box boards, but to sell them at a lower price so that it will be to Cuba's interest to import them in the future from that country. The owners of sawmills, victims of this ordinance, have since obtained its withdrawal, but too late, and only after the war will that export be able to resume some activity.

It was a few months after my return that the *cédula* or royal order finally arrived, which I mentioned in my memoir referred to the governor general, and which excluded the Spanish possessions in America from all commerce with foreigners. This order, against which all the officials of the province united, seemed to have been dictated by the Spanish court in order to alienate the feelings and obedience of the inhabitants in its colonies; more indeed, I believe, to favor the ambitions of the United States with regard to Louisiana if Spain were to keep it. The court ordered the merchants, whose ships have all been captured through lack of government protection, no longer to engage in supplying the colony with shipments under foreign flags on whatever pretext. And, since, under the terms of its last treaty with the United States, American ships had access to the Mississippi, it directed the warehousing of their cargoes so that they could be sold only in Spanish possessions where they had them transported. The effect was to force a contraband trade equipped to provide the colony's urgent needs. I would even dare to say to cause a widespread revolt; but the question was quite simple and local officials had the right to suspend, without exposing themselves to the least reproach, the execution of that order, as they effectively did.

The intendant, however, expressly hesitated to suspend the order, not wanting to expose himself for the welfare of the colony nor to run the risk of the slightest reprimand from the court. Fortunately, one of those men whose passion, pride, and fits of anger on all other occasions, nearly always result in their being dismissed as the head of a government, had been sent, as interim military governor, by the captain general of Cuba, to which Louisiana is subordinate, to put an end to the pretensions of various officers. That officer, vested with the powers of governor general, who might have caused mutiny in the colony by his haughtiness and vehemence, did more than the other officials in pronouncing himself strongly in favor of suspending the *cédula*, since they had not been able to contradict the obvious fact that the sending of the royal order had been only an error in the case of Louisiana, nor to contravene the list of misfortunes that would befall all of its inhabitants.

All the various groups of the colony made known their views. The business community asked me to present theirs, which I did with as much zeal as promptness in a manner that I deemed also essential for the peace of the colony. Besides the flattery that must be shown to monarchs and their representatives, I submitted a concise and true list of grievances and the obstructions to which the prosperity of the colony had been subjected. I received some flattering thanks from the business community and even from several government officials, but the intendant to whom my remarks were addressed, playing the role of merciless demigod, always seemed ready to hurl the thunderbolt with which His Majesty had armed him; but most fortunately, I repeat, the military governor vigorously pronounced himself in favor of suspension, and the intendant no longer thundered.

The interim governor general still continued in office, but the court finally replaced the incumbent [Morales] in the intendancy. It had for several years been in the hands of a "Hard Worker" for whom the art of riskless speculation in royal paper money had already assured a fortune; but in his administration, finding always the ordinances that restrained and never those that favored the prosperity and growth of a colony, he can lay claim to the rank as one of the foremost extortioners in all the Spanish possessions, and he should never be included among the list of real administrators.[10] The court approved of him, and that is as it should be if in Spain the administration is as it is in Louisiana: more severe and inquisitorial than beneficial. And, furthermore, more rarely in the colonies, as in all other places, will a Spanish financier try to merit in his affairs the esteem and understanding of the public and their regrets at losing him.

His successor, who had raised the hopes of the business community, soon ceased to offer any benefit from the change which had been made.[11] Various opportunities presented themselves that could have been of use to the colony in encouraging its commerce and agriculture, but it was always in vain. Some arrangements, as blameworthy as they were arbitrary, threw the royal treasury into a state of destitution that no longer permitted the making of the least payment in specie. He rejected the offers that were made by the business community to come to the aid of the colony in that regard. He hindered to such an extent, by his ordinances in wartime, the importation of slaves which the government had just approved, so that not a single local planter could take advantage of this authorization, and only one business firm in Europe, aware of this matter, had the time to solicit and to obtain an exclusive privilege, of which it has never made use. These odious measures encouraged, to the detriment of commerce, a large amount of speculation in the royal paper money, and again left agriculture without an increase in laborers when other Spanish colonies were receiving, by way of neutral ships, the slaves necessary for their prosperity.

Such was the state of affairs. The military or civil employee moaned, and commerce would certainly have only vegetated, as before, if the waters of the Mississippi had not brought, as I have already mentioned, the means to maintain its activity; means well above those which the Spanish settlements can furnish at this moment and which have already enriched Lousiana in spite of the mistakes and harassments of its administration.

The summary which I drew up of Louisiana at the time of my arrival in 1796, and which began these observations, is precisely factual. What I undertake to draw up today is already quite different, but it is not to the government that it owes its improvement. On the contrary, the government, by its neglect, has hampered commercial operations as much as it was within its power. The entire colony has often languished, and its own employees have often been deprived of their wages by neglecting to provide a convoy for the funds allocated to it. Since that time there have never been less that 600,000 piastres owed to Louisiana, and when the new intendant suddenly resigned his position, he left the royal treasury completely empty. It was from the resources of the often humiliated and vexed businessman, and from among the planters ignored in misery and left to their own devices, that the administrators then drew their needed funds. What a difference for the colony and what rights to the gratitude of its population, had Spanish funds always been regularly forwarded, and wisely used, and had they become a secondary support for its prosperity. One will appreciate how far the economy could have advanced and what advantage it could have gained, since despite its squanderings which are perhaps not less than 200,000 piastres a year, Louisiana did not owe a million at a time when 1,600,000 was due it. What encouragements for its commerce and agriculture! What facilities, as useful as well as agreeable, would they not be able to set up with the balance due their treasury, especially in a city like New Orleans where nothing is set aside for its police and sanitation.

Finally, at the time I write (March, 1802), the intendant, after having so often humiliated the business community by contempt for its protests, has just coerced it into refusing to assemble as a body to avoid his oppression as much as possible. The coming of peace, and a simple commentary on an arbitrary interpretation by the finance official regarding a beneficial order of the king to permit the export of specie, brought on new threats of persecution. Resigning themselves to being hampered in their operations, the businessmen have voluntarily given up as illusory the privilege of forming a chamber of commerce.

If the disturbing proceedings of the intendant had as their goal the prevention of fraud in connection with the customs duties which revert to the sovereign, far be it from me to have protested against an act of severity that I myself would invoke for the honor and fidelity of commerce in all its transactions; but the direct threat was only against imports. It seemed dangerous to him that there were such a large quantity of imports to which Spain never contributed, but on which she nevertheless always levied duties. Her conduct in hampering imports to the positive detriment of the treasury is new proof of my assertion about the secret plan to have the province stagnate, by not encouraging the movement of its products and supplies during peace, and by refusing to give it protection during war. Such is the effect of that pretended favor to Louisiana by the court of Spain, by permitting it to carry on trade with foreign countries, and by apparently not treating it with that political and religious severity which makes her other colonies tremble.

Will one believe that, from the news of the peace preliminaries, we have a commerce absolutely isolated from the favorable arrangements of its mother country and barred from carrying on trade with other Spanish colonies, owes to malice or the determination to impoverish and to discredit it, the information that when the actual treaty goes into effect cargoes coming from the United States will not be admitted?[12] But will they at least grant a delay of two months so that the foreigner, who has supplied us during the war under the shelter of his neutrality, can withdraw his funds? No! But will they, as a favor make an exception for the shipments en route, that have originated in part from the instructions and with the funds of New Orleans businessmen? No! These shipments will pay, without being in anyway harmful to the interests of the king, the fees that the treasury loses through the deposit! The business situation here is different from that of other colonies; we cause no harm to the commerce of the mother country which never deigned to concern herself to feed us, clothe us, and purchase our products. No! No! No! May the local authorities become more tractable when the definitive treaty arrives.

Such, I repeat, are the arrangements on which the commerce of Louisiana has been able at all times to establish its operations. Always stimulated by a seeming concession, nearly always the victim of an arbitrary hindrance from officials, or a deliberate plan of the court, the businessman can never allow that expansion of credit and purchases in his affairs for which a protected agriculture could provide the security. It is

57

not past nor even contemporary history of the commerce of Louisiana that I am trying to describe; I have only been able to indicate its origin. I would almost be compelled to say that during the first year of my residence there were not any businessmen at New Orleans, but generally only some small traders or cargo handlers selling at retail, more often to local merchants who sold in even smaller quantities for the convenience of the consumer. If I searched in vain for that chamber of commerce which had made me one of the syndics, the reasons which caused it to cease to exist should necessarily have occurred to me; and I believe that I had to give the foregoing account, so that the chamber's nonexistence for such a long time cannot reflect on the actual means whereby the soil and the colony's situation might have given it some life.

Trade with the Indians, about which I shall speak later, nevertheless established several businessmen and made their fortune, even during the time of the Spaniards, through the need to furnish an outlet for the pelts of these Indians, and to keep them in check, by providing supplies in exchange. But had I limited myself to presenting only the results of commerce in previous years without mentioning the reasons for its inactivity, a few lines would have sufficed. I would have recounted a condition of supplying and exportation that for thirty years, having largely diminished rather than augmented, had confirmed the accepted opinion of the scarcity of resources in the colony. In order to try to cover up the barrenness of such a narrative, I would have enumerated with some emphasis the bolts of linen and wool, the assortments of foodstuffs, scrap iron, hardware, china, and the various articles useful to the Indians; all the items, in fact, which the businessman or peddler of New Orleans could import from the three ports of France at which Spain, in her generosity, allowed them to call.[13] I would have observed that through a coastwide trade still permitted by the mother country, Saint-Domingue furnished indirectly a part of these supplies, and I would not have neglected to say that the island of Jamaica, and others, were selling the miserable remnants of Negro cargoes which supplied the slave quarters.

These imports, that necessity required, and for which Carondelet opened the way through the United States, were hampered in turn because the administration did not feel as he did the urgency to oppose the policy of the mother country regarding Louisiana. Those imports, I say, could still have offered an inducement for a European power to send their manufactured goods. But alas, what disinterestedness had not the statistics of exports inspired, rapidly approaching nullity, and presenting nothing more than the physical certainty of what Spain wanted: the neglect of a colony which, through the stagnation of a French population at the mouth of the Mississippi, assured a vast desert between the United States and Mexico.[14] Time and circumstances have frustrated Spain's projects without having yet made her realize the need to change policies. But despite the deep-seated conviction that I have of the local resources in Louisiana when she will encourage commerce and agriculture, I might never have dared to submit my ideas in this regard if the United States, by the accomplishments of their settlements beyond the Alleghenies, had not soon been able to provide in reality some of the advantages, which offered as future possibilities, would only pass for dreams.

Commerce, such as I have described it at the time of my arrival, has thus expanded itself as a result of these initial advantages, in a rapid enough progression to have considerably increased its exports. In 1796, it had perhaps not received from the western territory of the United States more than 1,200 barrels of flour, and this same country shipped supplies to the colony by sea; while in 1801, it exported to Louisiana, from Kentucky and the back countries of Pennsylvania, more than 50,000 barrels of flour, making up the deficit in the colony's requirements. Tobacco and rope have increased almost in the same proportion; and from the banks of the Mississippi and several of its branches in the same year, Louisiana offered the United States in exchange more than 15,000 bales of cotton, more than 1,000 boxes of raw sugar, some indigo, pelts, and so on. Such then would have been the progressive growth if the war, hampering all operations, had not prevented the speculator in Kentucky, and in other territories equally fertile, from finding a market at New Orleans as ready as it was advantageous for commodities, in the cultivation of which the planters, if encouraged, might have been more persevering and daring. What an increase in wealth would not New Orleans have derived from land under control of its government in shipping to the tropical colonies its lumber, tar, rosin, masts, and other products, and in selling to its advantage in the European markets the old indigo that commerce and its planters were holding back for the advent of peace, as well as the plug tobacco which Spain had discontinued importing.

It is possible to visualize the colony's growth by the experience of this year [1802], which already feels the advantages of a peace which the hero of France [Napoleon Bonaparte] seems to want to assure to Europe and America. The waterways of the Mississippi have brought to the New Orleans market 30,000 more barrels of flour than in the preceding year; they will provide there, in addition, 12,000 to 15,000 bales of cotton and at least 3 million pounds of raw sugar. The receipts of the pelts in actual fact have been negligible because of corrupt supervision, on which I shall elaborate when discussing trade with the Indians. New harvests of indigo have also been insignificant for many years. The low price of tobacco has reduced its export. The production of cordage has not been sufficient to meet the demands of government and individuals, and especially to supply the large consumption which the baling of cotton has required. Salt pork and

salt beef, which they had not yet offered for ex\
finally been produced in considerable quantities;\
unique result of the peace preliminaries, all these\
have avoided the ruinous effects of the deposit\
protracted warehousing to which an uncertain shippi\
ation previously forced them. Starting in January\
February [1802], the port of New Orleans, filled with three
rows of ships, presented the spectacle of a forest of masts,
unheard-of up to now, that reduced in April and May only in
assuring the end of the colony's stagnation and the certainty
of its future prosperity. And newly arrived vessels, loaded in
ballast, have generally taken the place of others, and have
assured that every spring and summer the New Orleans
warehouses will have numerous cargoes either to exchange
for imports or to load as freight for Europe and the Antilles.

The other domestic resources of Lower Louisiana have not
yet been able to be made profitable by the benefits of pacifica-
tion in Europe, nor to increase the amount of exports this
year. Rosin and tar, lumber of every kind, Natchitoches
tobacco, rice, and other items would soon complete the
assortment of products; and I can repeat here the prophecy
that I made regarding the advantages and wealth of the New
Orleans market in my memoir of 1798. There, as I said with
some admiration, one will see the coming together of all the
products of the Temperate Zones with the much larger
number from the Torrid Zones. Ships in great numbers will
discharge simultaneously on her fortunate shores cargoes of
sugar, flour, indigo, salt provisions, cotton, hemp, rope, pelts,
lead, lumber of every kind, iron, rice, and tobacco.

The list of commercial imports has not been any less
astonishing. Rich and varied cargoes have replaced the small
number and mediocrity of those that it received, for which
the land produced almost nothing in exchange. In that same
year, 1796, the consumption of imported goods could have
been at the most a million piastres, and commerce had then,

as a pledge for its credit and encouragement of its operations only the misery of the planter. Now it has imported not less than three million piastres, which agriculture, as I will prove shortly in much greater detail, can already pay for with its products. Finally, the businessmen, storekeepers, and peddlers have increased in numbers. Some important business houses of the United States have already become silent partners in local firms, with guarantees of the greatest security. Several from Europe, in fact, will rival them in success, and one sees prevailing everywhere the affluence that comes to a country which enriches itself, and the expectation of wealth that it promises.

I end here, subject to the political summary that I shall offer, my *Observations* insofar as they may concern commerce. I have expanded them into such details, particularly the administrators' conduct, only to justify what I have said with respect to the precariousness of the colony's existence. I have emphasized the hindrances that have been raised up against it, to correct the erroneous information which they advanced regarding the degree of prosperity that Louisiana has already reached, in imagining that it is only the result of the Spanish government's favors. I wanted to prove, in that regard, that the court of Spain has acted, or that its representatives have almost always caused it to act, as though, by premeditated design, it wanted only the survival without growth of the French who lived on the banks of the Mississippi. Finally, I sought to prove—as its belated progress now swiftly and splendidly growing will show—that it owes all its local improvements to the courage of its inhabitants and its location; and that it is exclusively to foreigners, whom a beneficial chance brought to the upper reaches of the Mississippi's left bank, that Louisiana owes the inexhaustible flow of prosperity which will overcome, as it spreads in its course, all of the obstacles that they wanted to place in its path.

CHAPTER FOUR

Agriculture

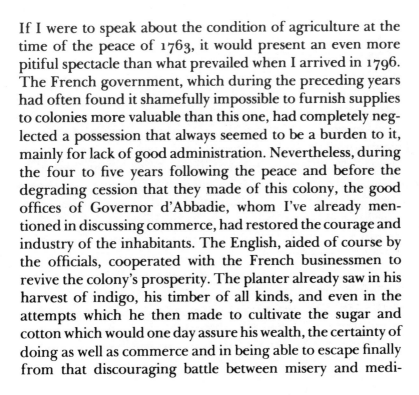

If I were to speak about the condition of agriculture at the time of the peace of 1763, it would present an even more pitiful spectacle than what prevailed when I arrived in 1796. The French government, which during the preceding years had often found it shamefully impossible to furnish supplies to colonies more valuable than this one, had completely neglected a possession that always seemed to be a burden to it, mainly for lack of good administration. Nevertheless, during the four to five years following the peace and before the degrading cession that they made of this colony, the good offices of Governor d'Abbadie, whom I've already mentioned in discussing commerce, had restored the courage and industry of the inhabitants. The English, aided of course by the officials, cooperated with the French businessmen to revive the colony's prosperity. The planter already saw in his harvest of indigo, his timber of all kinds, and even in the attempts which he then made to cultivate the sugar and cotton which would one day assure his wealth, the certainty of doing as well as commerce and in being able to escape finally from that discouraging battle between misery and mediocrity. Hope for the future banished from all hearts the remembrance of past privations, and, happy to call themselves Frenchmen, they resisted for a long time facing up to the crime that Versailles committed in their regard.[1] Even after having learned it officially, they thought that upon the withdrawal of Ulloa, the first Spanish governor, their deputies would receive justice from a sovereign whose courtiers had made him commit an act of cowardice.[2] Their courage and labors were enhanced by the patriotism which they vividly demonstrated to their mother country; and from that moment the colony would have taken all the steps of which it was then capable had France listened to its wishes. They were, alas, deceived in their expectations. Another Spanish official, or rather a tiger (O'Reilly) in the service of that power, came to take possession in the name of his sovereign. Their cries and protestations were not heeded by the French government and, to its eternal shame, six among them—with the overflow of love which the entire colony had manifested for France—died [1769] before a firing squad.

It would not take much trouble for one to imagine what effect this event produced. Discouragement was widespread, and powerless to avenge the unfortunate victims of France's abandonment, I would almost venture to say Spanish savagery, the colonists did nothing more than only wish they could leave the colony. If, in the destruction of its commerce and agriculture, the city and countryside were not deserted, it was because of lack of buyers. For in the state of stupor and terror into which O'Reilly had thrown the population, they offered at ridiculous prices properties which before his arrival seemed to assure the happiness of families and the wealth of the colony.

To O'Reilly, whose stay fortunately was not long enough to achieve the entire ruin of the colony, had succeeded, up to the time of my arrival, several officials who generally did not depart from the pilfering ideas of a colonial governor. The first was Unzaga [1770–1776] who as intendant and governor gave some luster to agriculture by closing his eyes to the contraband trade with the English, owners at that time of the left bank of the Mississippi from its source down to the boundaries of Lower Louisiana.[3] Their ships—to the detriment of a local commerce that the Spanish government had destroyed and for the reestablishment of which they were taking no initiative—brought some Negroes and provisions which they supplied to the planter at a low price. They gave him considerable credit and received in payment all that the soil placed at his disposal in lumber and commodities, however small the article might be.

The Spanish government wanted to appear at times as occupying itself with the prosperity of the colony, by granting some favors which certain incidents or subsequent orders rendered useless. Such, for example, was the permission granted to supply the island of Cuba with sugar boxes which it needed and which, added to the outlets that the island of Saint-Domingue offered for all the lumber that was brought there, favored the establishment of sawmills on both banks of the river. Such was, also, the encouragement given under royal decree to grow tobacco, and the king undertook to buy annually a considerable amount. Such were, finally, several attempts to increase the population which like the others served for a while to mask the determination to make the country vegetate rather than flourish.

What became of these marvelous encouragements on the part of the government? First: The king's order was not exactly carried out in Havana where they transported the boxes. The manufacturer of the boxes encountered some difficulties for which he felt obliged to blame his supplier in Lower Louisiana, and the latter—against whom the Anglo-Americans also raised the loudest complaints in Saint-Domingue regarding the stave wood, and timber—soon saw his stocks rotting. Second: By an abominable fraud the administration, which ought to buy from the Louisiana planter the full amount of tobacco contracted for the king, sometimes filled it in large part out of the initial attempts at tobacco cultivation coming from the settlements of the United States along the [Ohio] river in Kentucky. And the local planter, being cheated, was obliged to sell his own tobacco to individuals at a low price. Moreover, the mother country—which never thought that she should essentially concern herself with this colony—discontinued [1792] taking that tobacco, and, not offering any indemnity to the unfortunate colonist, seemed to doom him to his original misery. Third: Finally, the families that immigrated to these shores— one group from the Canary Islands, known here by the name of Islanders, another of Acadian refugees in Brittany whom France released and several families from New England— were thrown upon, rather than transported to, the soil of Louisiana. The expenses which the government undertook in that regard enriched several individuals, and did not turn to the advantage of the immigrants, who were practically living, without exception, in the most profound misery at the time of my arrival. In fact, how could they have prospered under a government that hampered domestic commerce in all sorts of ways, while not importing from its mother country any supplies, nor exporting to its profit any of the soil's products? In addition, the government discontinued tolerating contraband trade even before necessity required it, and occupied itself, always only at the last moment and with a tax collector's parsimony, in attempts to correct the vices of such an administration.

It was by these means, of which I present here only an outline, that they brought agriculture to the condition, as poor as it was distressing, in which I found it. With more to complain about than commerce—to which the piastres of the government finally reimbursed its advances, and which was creditor of the planters with its profits—agriculture had seen

66

the sustenance and fruits of its labors periodically suppressed. It did not have, as did commerce, the ability and occasion to buy in order to engage in smuggling, nor the means to make good its losses. Everything seemed to have conspired to destroy agriculture: insects, devastating floods, and hurricanes, all in fact walked abreast with the government to impoverish the colony. The planter existed only in difficulties and privations; he was riddled with debts and exhausted by the wasteful weariness of current griefs and anxiety for the future. Moreover, he was not harvesting anything, or harvested for many years only things without value; and he was tormented finally by the political situation in Europe, the restlessness of which reacted upon him by making it impossible to replace the slaves taken by death. This was, in 1796, the condition generally of agriculture in Lower Louisiana and the communities in the upper reaches which, too remote from the benefits of the Indian trade, had taken up the growing of tobacco.

The progress of agriculture, as well as its decay, in Upper Louisiana can only be touched on briefly. The measures that were taken against equity, proper supervision, population, and politics, subjected the communities of that region to tyranny and monopoly at all times. Peltry was always the only product which they concerned themselves with before that time, but that trade diminished because of the distance to the locality where the Indians have withdrawn, and where it is necessary to go in order to trade with them. Moreover, the colony's generally bad administration, multiplying the obstacles to and forging chains on domestic commerce, robbed it of the necessary means and energy to carry on a successful Indian trade. This forced the company that dependably undertook this trading to sell to the enemy or its ally, without any advantage to the colony, all the choice pelts and even a portion of those from bears and deer.[4] Nevertheless, peltry is the only article of export that continued, because when the cession of Louisiana by France took place the trading population already existed on the spot. And the Spanish government, hardly interested in increasing the fur trade, was satisfied to maintain it and to send military commanders to Upper Louisiana in order to enrich themselves. These military commanders have seen a population of the United States established on the banks of the Ohio without emulating it, even though they possess a better soil which, unlike the American side, no longer had to be protected by force of arms. Moreover, they have seen, in silence and apathy, that population increase daily and settle, in the space of twenty years, communities as widespread as they are productive, which will not always be content to enrich, in spite of the military commanders, the major portion of the Upper Louisiana colonists still subject to their authority.

I shall not speak here of the measures which Spain should have undertaken long ago to improve agriculture in the province of Louisiana, and to prepare in advance for the competition that all European governments ought to give to the United States for possession of Louisiana. But I shall have occasion to dwell at length on this matter when I deal with its political relationships and topography.

To sum up, at the time of my arrival—the point from where I generally start to present my *Observations on Louisiana* —what did agriculture offer to the languishing commerce that supported it? Indigo: Several harvests were realized on lands in some manner so favored, since for several years the soil, bad weather, and insects worked against its successful cultivation in the arable portion of Lower Louisiana. It soon fell, however, to such a low price that no one any longer wanted to run the many risks of being a victim of indigo.

Rice: The cultivation of which they had attempted to undertake, but for two to three piastres a barrel at the most. It offered so few advantages to the planter that to continue its cultivation even at that price he could send it to market only to buy a sufficient amount of goods for his urgent needs.

Rosin and tar: The creditor commercial interests and the buyer not being able to obtain from the administration permission to export these products freely to the other Spanish colonies where they are sold advantageously, and the ship having no hope of any protection at all in wartime, those who engaged in this trade were soon obliged to abandon it.

Sawed timber and stave wood: The war with England prevented their being produced and (like the two preceding articles) the ships of the United States, the only ones that could sometimes engage in trade without fear, could not take them on for shipment to their country since they themselves export these products to foreign countries in competition with this province.

Ship masts: This item can be mentioned in the list of Louisiana's resources, but what is exported is usually for the account of the king who, by contract, makes the fortune of a private individual and sees that he receives the supplies from Havana that he has ordered. This export is still only precarious and in some years is often nonexistent.

Sugar box boards for Havana: The Spanish ships carrying this export were soon captured by the enemy; and the administration, by a kind of persistence in hindering things, prohibited their exportation in American vessels. The boards rotted on the spot, as often happened in other circumstances and for other reasons, and brought about the ruin and despair of the owner. And when exportation was again permitted in American ships, which they had thought necessary to prohibit, he was able to sell only at a low price what the termites had not already consumed. The exporter himself no longer realized any profit because the ships of the United States, having gone directly from their country to the island of Cuba, transported a very large quantity of their own boards.

Plug tobacco: Its production had been encouraged by a

contract to fill the needs of the mother country, but the king or his agents suspended their purchases. In recent years the tobacco planter offered it for quite a while to merchants, but they could not handle it profitably. He finally sold it at distress prices to cover his expenses, and retired to the bosom of his family where he could hide his misery and chagrin.

Lead: It came from the Illinois country where they hardly mined enough for the needs of the colony. Nothing had yet been done to find an extensive use for this metal, either in casting or in rolling, and the excess of what came down to New Orleans already served to provide the needs of the settlements of the United States along the Ohio and Kentucky rivers, and other localities.

Peltry: Here then, at last, is the only trade that combines the needs of the Indian and the habits of the old colonist in the distant settlements, who prefers to be a hunter and boatman than a farmer. It has again suffered a large decrease in profit for the colony, only because of the route that traders are required to take as a result of the commercial obstacles. That is, by placing the upper settlements in the position of receiving supplies at a better price by the short cut through the United States, and by requiring, for their greater advantage, the sending of their best skins and those of lower grades to Canada and sometimes even as far as Fort Pitt. Finally, this trade consisted of about 100,000 pounds in weight of shorn deer skins, 180,000 pounds of unshorn skins of the same animal, an almost insignificant quantity of skins from otters, beavers, bears, buffalo, wildcats—which altogether could amount to as much as 200,000 piastres. Several business houses, which had assembled the assortment of peltries for those posts, or could ship them to England (the only profitable route that was open to them in view of the lack of ships and protection), divided these peltries among themselves to exchange for remaindered goods.

Indigo, rosin and tar, plug tobacco, boards for boxes, and

the attempts at producing sugar and cotton can be estimated at 200,000 piastres in that same year. Thus, the entire colony in its actual production offered at the most in 1796 only 400,000 piastres in exchange for its supplies. With what then did they balance the remittances for the colony's articles of general consumption? With the hard cash that Spain expected to be used for the payment of the troops and employees, and that of several ships from Vera Cruz and Campêche which happily came sometimes to exchange it fraudulently for merchandise, while also bringing dyewoods, some sugar, a little cochineal, and vanilla. With the excess of the sugar for the needs of the colony, imported from Havana in exchange for boxes; with some tobacco in hogsheads that the settlements of the United States already were sending; and finally, with nothing else than firewood to cover and hide the sacks of piastres, when it was not possible to secure any article for export, a harsh experience which I myself had that same year. I do not include here the tafia, rum, and coffee of which there was hardly ever any excess for reexportation to other colonies. These means of remittances to Europe or the United States did not in any way relieve the situation of the planter. On the contrary, he thought that he could envy the businessman who in turn—when these same methods did not work, either through frequent delay in remittances of funds or the severity of administrators (as much in this colony as in similar ones), or finally because of the weather—complained about the adversities of trade. Moreover, the businessman suffered humiliation in receiving complaints from his principals or suppliers who accused him of misusing their funds to his profit.

The unfortunate planter who saw the businessman scheming with apparent success amid all the difficulties, not only had to bemoan the paucity of his revenues, but still dwelled on it when they were about to be totally eliminated either through the worthlessness of various commodities or because the soil refused to produce others, or because war finally made it impossible to export those that seemed to be his last resource. He was going to vegetate miserably if some courageous men, among even those whose labors for a long time had been the least productive, had not had recourse to a fresh attempt at cultivating some valuable products which, abandoned since the Spaniards took possession, were thought to have been failures. I refer to cotton and sugar, to which the planters of Louisiana owe their present wealth and without which they would be, with few exceptions, I repeat, all in a miserable state at a time when commerce found itself, as it were, supplied by the rapid increase of the products which come down to New Orleans from the settlements of the United States on the banks of the Mississippi.

Cotton was then replanted in the colony, and the first efforts in that new cultivation were guided rather by necessity than hope of success, since tradition regarding earlier attempts could serve to discourage it. Nevertheless, agreeably surprised with the results, their labor—far from being lost as it had been for many years in the crops of indigo—was rewarded. Immediately followed by those who through fear, preoccupation, or discouragement of misfortune had kept in idleness, they saw an annual increase in the products of a soil that was thought worn-out, and gins and presses were established and improved for the exploitation of that commodity. They harvested about one thousand pounds of seed cotton per arpent [.85 acre], and cultivated at least three arpents with each laborer. Ease then finally took the place of want among a great many planters, and wealth soon banished financial embarrassment and privations among several others. Circumstances made the price of cotton increase and stay at the highest level; and in a country where a few years earlier agriculture did not provide enough for commerce to half fill the small number of ships that brought in the colony's supplies, one saw a growing number coming in ballast to take on cargo.

While that revolution was going on [1790s] and in general spreading its benefits over most of the colony's planters, sugarcane had occasioned another one for those widely scattered among the lands of Lower Louisiana from the mouth of the river as far as fifty leagues above, who by reason of the climate and their manpower could cultivate it with success. Nature, in short, gave to cotton, as it did throughout the tropics, the one commodity that could supplement its exportation.

In 1795, an active and enterprising planter—who had exhausted all the means of continuing the cultivation of indigo, and had suffered more from this crop than anyone else—resolved to establish and undertake on a large scale the cultivation of sugarcane. The year before, another planter with little means and aided by day laborers had realized a modest income by making syrup and converting it into tafia; and this feeble attempt, by reason of the prejudice against such cultivation, might have languished many more years and perhaps even died out.[5] For sugar to turn to the great advantage of the colony, it was necessary that a daring man undertake its production; and the person about whom I want to speak—despite the new financing that he had to take on for the equipment, and despite his family's protests, the advice of his friends, and even the observations of numerous acquaintances whom the loyalty of his character has always attracted to him—planned early in that year a large establishment; he planted 100 arpents of cane to be harvested into sugar in 1796, paid a high price to be certain of having a sugarmaker, built the grinding shed, sugar mill, drying house, and sheds, and to the astonishment of the entire province made, with about thirty Negroes, 100,000 pounds of raw sugar. The first attempts of the previous year had already encouraged some others who also made a little money, but in 1797 there was in increase in sugar mills, and if establishments of this type have been limited to about fifty, it is because there is a lack of workers due to the ban on the importation of Negroes.

Before summarizing the advantages which the colony has gained from that cultivation, I think that I should speak about the quality of sugar they have produced up to this time; five years of experience not having irrevocably fixed the opinion of commerce in its favor, and not having been able then to encourage the planter who could undertake but nevertheless, has not yet undertaken, an establishment of that nature. If I am permitted to give my opinion based upon the knowledge which ten years of residence on sugar plantations in Saint-Domingue placed me in the position of acquiring, I shall affirm that one can make fine and good sugar in this colony, barring (as can also happen in the tropics) an excess of rain or a dry spell, and barring also a freeze which in unusual years can damage the uncut cane. And if I do not doubt that a good sugar producer can grow sugar in Louisiana less subject to decomposition than is that of the Torrid Zones, I must acknowledge that by the nature of the soil and climate, the cane, having an early maturity more apparent than real, cannot stand the carelessness in production which was often permitted in other countries—especially in sugar mills producing only raw sugar. Because of that situation I am convinced that all the defective sugars which are produced and which, to the temporary disadvantage of the colony have been exported, are in that condition only through lack of care in production, or because a planter, by laziness or want of foresight, allowed the standing cane to freeze, and has persisted in making sugar out of it rather than turning it only into syrup.

The first buyers in the United States contributed not a little to the planters' mistakes by demanding sugar of them, deluded into thinking that the cane would live up to expectations. From another angle, pride has blinded many persons who, at the sight of a product favored by the weather in its thickening rather than in its crystallization, thought that they had made fine merchandise. They had in fact barreled only a molasses thickened in appearance, but filled with foreign particles which turns it sour as a result of fermentation when warm. Thus, the buyer, who as an expert has a sugarmaker's pride, is completely deceived in his speculation. Neglecting to skim the juice, which, because of the cane's richness in very hot climates, does not have as many foreign particles, can, in itself and even with a good sugarmaker, cause a sort of decomposition in the sugar of this country during warm weather. For that reason, the sugarmaker needs to take greater pains here, as the cane juice requires close attention and cautious handling. He should not spoil, by a deficiency of lime, a cane juice too weak in its maturity to be able to tolerate a residue of acid or gum without danger; he should handle the skimming with the same attention as if he were making white sugar, that is to say, to be bleached and dried. But he should also guard against making it too thin by an excess of alkali, too thick by overcooking, or separating, by too little cooking, the texture of a sugar of fine and good quality which he can produce by his carefulness, and in which the raw material does not acquire enough richness so that one can handle it with the negligence common in climates more adapted to the cultivation of sugarcane.

That is what I think of sugar in Louisiana; and if, contrary to all probability, the cultivation was ever abandoned, it will be because of not having avoided the mistakes to which I have just referred. If, by reason of the soil or proper planting, the quantity exceeds the expectations that they had originally conceived, and an arpent of cane often yields from its first planting between 2,500 and 3,000 pounds of sugar, and if, despite the fact that the experience of several shipments has proven the contrary, the raw sugar of Louisiana in crossing the ocean should become decomposed, it would nevertheless be a fact that cultivation could in the future continue to increase, as it has in the past, the planters' wealth. This will happen when the importation of Negroes will provide all the manpower necessary to handle their bleached and refined sugars, which they can then dry and ship across the ocean, whenever they so desire, to rival the sugar of other countries.

I should also say something about the quality of the cotton, but if I spoke with the severity of a man who compared it impartially to the cotton of Saint-Domingue, Cayenne, and other places, I would probably be contradicted by the experience of European manufacturers who, without valuing it as much as those I have just mentioned, nevertheless know how to make the most of it, and have bid for it in the markets of England as much as fifty sols tournois a pound.[6] I shall note also, to its credit, that it is quite silky and white, and the soil does not produce it with as short a staple as when it is exported so that it loses considerably in that regard by the faulty cleaning machines that damage the cotton in the seed by shaving it, rather than separating one from the other without that disadvantage. They say everywhere that the price of sugar will fall in this province. I believe it, and cotton will also fall in price. But if a fortunate circumstance has placed the planter in the position of getting out of debt, and if during several years he has earned 15, 20, and 25 percent on his capital, do they believe that to maintain his prosperity it is indispensible that he always realize a profit at that rate? No, and if that was the case, Louisiana would soon yield in wealth to no other country in the world. But, be that as it may, sugar at seven sols tournois and cotton at twenty-five could fall in price by 33 percent, and yet not cause the wealth and splendor of the colony to cease to expand.

If, to offer a contrast to the poverty and destitution of the colony in 1796, we summarize what the harvest of 1801 will have given to commerce in exchange for its imported supplies, we would first of all have some indigo from previous years harvests—which the wealthier inhabitants have kept off the market in anticipation of peace and which should be included for the record only as economies of former times— amounting to about a million piastres. Rice—which at present is cultivated only for local consumption and which at the price of eight piastres a barrel makes its planter as wealthy as any other commodity—will not be included in the current list of exports. Rosin, tar, lumber, stave wood, planks for sugar boxes, masts, plug tobacco, lead, and other commodities still amount to almost nothing, for the reasons given when referring to the products of 1796. They will appear here as an offset to the cotton coming from the communities in the United States, for which the commerce of New Orleans, because of the imports by way of the Ohio, will not have furnished all the products to balance the payments.

Thus, we will actually start with peltry which can always be estimated at the same amount of 200,000 piastres. We will add at least 8 million pounds of cotton (including that from Natchez and Cumberland in the territory of the United States) which at 20 sols makes a sum of 1,600,000 piastres; and finally we will add about 6 million pounds of sugar that we will value at 6 sols a pound, which amounts to 360,000 piastres. Those three amounts together will give a total of 2,160,000 piastres which is greater than the domestic production when I arrived of 1,760,000 piastres. And the articles eliminated by the war will considerably increase that balance soon after the first years of peace, in compensating even for the drop in prices that could be sustained by the other commodities. I have not included molasses in this estimate, a quantity of which was exported during the early years, but which now made into tafia by the distilleries that are established, fills the needs of the country and converts into a profit

77

for the colony the funds that it paid to Havana in order to obtain it.

If we then come back to the possible articles which completed the exchangeable items that made up commerce in 1796, and in the listing of which we have previously gone into, to begin with we will find cash—the result of economies referred to in my comments on commerce—amounting to at least 600,000 piastres in spite of squandering the funds allocated for this colony and still due from the viceroy of Mexico. Then follows: (1) Vera Cruz, which no longer exports more than a small amount of sugar to Louisiana, but which in so doing brings more silver to finance the purchases of its contraband trade; (2) Campêche, which exports considerably less of its dyewoods to the colony because of the lack of ships and government protection; (3) Havana, which has considerably reduced the exportation of its refined sugars and tafia to Louisiana, and soon will be able to offer only coffee for sale there; and, finally, (4) the settlements of the United States along the Ohio, which are those that are going to replace what Louisiana should have been able to import in its relations with Campêche, Vera Cruz, and Havana. Their last year's harvest provided for export in flour and tobacco to Louisiana at least 500,000 piastres. It is a matter of common knowledge that the favorable prices they obtained for their flour have made them more than triple production. Moreover, aside from the Natchez cotton that I have included among the domestic output of the Spanish territories because they have depended on it up to this day through commercial relationships, those settlements will provide for the use of the province the following items: flour, hemp, twine, salt provisions, fats, and so on, totaling 700,000 to 800,000 piastres. Thus an aggregate of 3 million piastres to exchange for exports, without including any of the articles which the war had hampered, nor the controlled specie and the current revenues that are granted to it by the government.

After having established that difference in situation with respect to agriculture, as I have previously done regarding commerce, I shall ask the Spanish government if it can flatter itself with having contributed anything to that improvement? Has it ever made, by its care or its encouragements, any attempt to secure for the planters the objects they needed, any preferential treatment in taxes, any subsidy, compensations, advances; in short, has it inspired the courage and aroused the ambition of the planters, burdened down with debt, to whose labors and energy the colony owes its well-being? Has it, with better police protection and improved control in suppressing fugitive Negroes, assured to the owners the use of their slaves' working strength? Finally, when it saw a dying colony revived by the cultivation of sugar and cotton, has it effectively concerned itself with the means to increase these same workers without danger to the peace of the colony, and even without expense to the treasury? No, and I could ask a hundred similar questions that would always be answered in the negative. Several businessmen of the colony, aided by a large number of foreigners favored by the last treaty with the United States, alone have supplied the needs of the planters by their imports, and have in turn encouraged them by their purchases.[7] And when at the island of Cuba, so close to this colony, all of the nations in ships of Danish and Swedish registry increased by tenfold its agricultural production by bringing in Negroes, unfortunate Louisiana could not receive them and struggled on the edge of a precipice created by the contrariness of the land, fires, hurricanes, and floods, and by the calculated indifference of its government in all things that could have aided it.

CHAPTER FIVE

Trade with the Indians

Now is the proper time to refer to this subject, as I have just given the results of commerce and agriculture. The Indian trade concerns these two fine pursuits in quite different ways when it is not viewed in its true aspect. And because of the manner in which the Spanish government has dealt with this trade, it is a weak advantage for commerce and provides an obstacle in the way of improving agriculture in the settlements so situated as to be able to communicate with the Indians.

In discussing commerce I included peltry among the resources available for export, and then when referring to agriculture I have shown it in greater detail in my summary of the products of the land. Ever since Spain has owned the colony that article has undergone only imperceptible changes, but always to its disadvantage. Indifferent to the prosperity of a country, the simple possession of which was sufficient for her, she did not concern herself with the progress of the Indian trade, as necessary as it might be for the happiness and security of the province. Initially, the court made a contract with an English business house, about which

I have already spoken in my notes on agriculture, for trade with the Florida Indians. That firm located its branches in the interior of the country and on the Gulf of Mexico; it received its supplies from England at Pensacola, where it established its main office. By lavishing the gold and presents necessary to stifle domestic commerce and to conceal the unlawful acts that chance events would enable them to commit, it has enjoyed—up to the time when rearrangements of the borders with the United States eliminated several branch offices —an exclusive trade with the Indians on lands bounded to the south by the Gulf of Mexico, to the west by the Mississippi, to the north by the Ohio and Tennessee rivers, and to the east by the Bahama Channel [Florida east coast].

By isolating the Indian trade in the hands of foreigners, the court lost its right to the province's gratitude, which it could have earned by encouraging commercial interests to undertake this trade, and by even supporting them with necessary advances. Moreover, the officials of the colony in general did not take more prudent and effective initiatives to assure for their profit, and that of the treasury, the Indian trade in the upper settlements of the Mississippi and those which are being established on the tributaries of its right bank. The various privileges granted in that regard either ended in the hands of the military officer sent to command a post, the token of his illicit gains that assured his fortune, or resulted in addition to oppression of individuals by an annual assessment in favor of the chief official and his secretary. Nor did the colony's officials concern themselves to any degree with the supervision that should have assured products for the commerce of the province, as well as export fees for the treasury. All the choice pelts—beaver, otter, and others, and some of the skins of bears and deer—continually took the route to Canada by way of the Illinois River and other streams, and as is often the case made the Spanish settlements dependent on English prosperity.

The major portion of the inhabitants—without reflecting on the political consequences to commerce and on the necessity of not abandoning to chance the supplying of the Indian nations—have constantly wished that a freedom of trade, for whoever wanted to undertake it, might abolish all exclusive privilege, and in their opinion turn to the advantage of the settlements favorably situated to follow it. If the government agreed to this it would, I believe, result in a mistake much more harmful to the political interests of the province than the abuse that it still makes of the trading privileges. The laws that it enacts for monopolies are nearly always only an illusory condescension to the court decrees, and the so-called forts that are built for them are only miserable huts. And if the sole implied stipulation (illicit gain) is the only one that is completely carried through it is a fact that for their private interest the monopolies maintain, in making themselves respected, abundance and peace among the Indians and delay the enemy's progress in trading on territory of the province.

To give an exact idea of the manner in which I view trade with the Indian nations, I am going to copy word for word an opinion—of which I was the author at the earnest request of three other businessmen out of five who, along with me, were consulted officially by the governor general of the province—regarding trading privileges with the Indians. That consultation was occasioned by the petition which some of the inhabitants of Saint Louis in the Illinois country presented to the government requesting abolition of trading privileges. It was not out of respect that they asked our opinion, and the interests of commerce in New Orleans were not what worried the government. Besides, accustomed to enjoying only indirectly some profit from the Indian trade, the businessmen might have accepted its decision without complaint, but it consisted of nothing less than a move to eliminate a valuable source of incidental profits. In consulting with us, the government reserved for itself the right to support our opinion if it was worth the trouble, or to reject it by rebuking us if we dared to oppose the only objective they had: Masking their interests under the veil of public service. They convened us with the two chief finance officials and the military prosecutor.[1] These gentlemen smiled scornfully while avoiding a precise opinion, and we withdrew by promising to submit our views. We did so and four of us signed the report which I wrote and which I am going to quote here. Two of the businessmen, of a more fearful conscience regarding exclusive privileges, gave a separate opinion that did not come to my attention.

The Governor. Sir,
The undersigned have the honor to submit the opinion that you have requested from us regarding trading privileges with the Missouri Indians. If they had listened only to the first cry of innate fairness, the undersigned would also have raised their protests, because all exclusive privilege, in general, is repugnant to the maxims of a wise administration. But reflecting with mature consideration on the private individual's arrangements for trading with the Missouri Indians, and on the results of the freedom that would be granted to each person to undertake it, the undersigned are convinced that all means employed to take away from the inhabitant of the posts the occupation of isolated trade would be a good deed on the part of the government. That is: the hazards of the long voyage to reach the places where this trade is now carried on; the necessity to keep it entirely for the province despite the efforts being made by the English to take it over; the need to assure, by advancing money, the maintenance and reliability of a privileged person, peace with the unruly Indian tribes where trade is carried on, fees that are paid annually to the treasury, and supplies that this trade furnishes to the commerce of the colony; the advantage of urging to useful and safe labors most men who, to the misfortune of their families, would otherwise devote themselves to a vagabond and often debauched life which isolated traders are almost forced to lead among the Indians; the requirement, which the example of hard working neighbors seems to dictate, that they should turn

their sights and incentives toward agriculture; the experience of the stagnation of a population always poor in the proportion of one hundred to one, because the habits and training in the occupation of Indian trader have constantly moved it backwards toward the uncivilized life of the Indians; everything in the final analysis tends to make the undersigned believe that the best interest of the province of Louisiana is to invite the inhabitants of the distant posts to work at the cultivation of the fertile territory that surrounds them and make them, by encouragements in that regard, strangers as much as possible to the Indian trade; and, in this connection, the foregoing remarks are considered only under their political aspects for the maintenance of peace and the integrity of the rights of the province.

When the trade was carried on near the posts, it never enriched more than a few merchant tradesmen who periodically abandoned the other inhabitants, tools of their fortune, to an unchanging miserable way of life. Now that it is necessary to traverse 200, 300, or 400 leagues—with such additional hazards and annoyances that the large means of a privileged trade can hardly overcome—it would endanger the life of the isolated trader at every moment, the fortune of his employer, even the tranquility of the province, in order to avenge the murders and frequent pillages in which the Indians and alien traders engage. With widespread freedom of trade in the Illinois country, how can we prevent our neighbors on the opposite bank from taking the major portion of the trade for themselves? In transporting the pelts from those posts by way of the Ohio River to Fort Pitt, and by the Illinois River and other streams to Canada, they have already often deprived the province of its rights, and the undersigned do not doubt that soon the only pelts to reach New Orleans will be those recognized as being of American origin. These neighbors will also know how to supply secretly the trader or merchant, and by a step condemned by politics and in fact ruinous to the prosperity of the Spanish settlements, the English at the headwaters of the Missouri, and the Anglo-Americans on the bankes of the Mississippi, will take for themselves almost all the profit of the trade without improving the situation of the colonist.

The undersigned are far from believing that it might be

harmful to extend the trading privileges to a company instead of granting them to an individual. On the contrary, they envisage the advantage that could result for the province when several individuals might unite themselves in an enterprise of this kind that would offer to the government a much greater political and moral responsibility. Political, in that being better able to endure the uncertainties of furnishing supplies, the always contented Indians would be peaceful. And moral, because jealous to maintain trust in one another, several individuals in a company will be less able to carry on the reprehensible actions which enrich the foreign business houses, frustrate primarily the province's participation in the commercial transactions required by the Indian trade, and in turn take away from the sovereign the taxes that he should have collected.

The undersigned believe that this matter of tax collection requires the most careful supervision on the part of the government. And grateful for the expressions of your confidence, we beg of you to accept our wishes for your continued good health.

New Orleans
February 17, 1802

If Spain had essentially wanted to concern herself with encouraging several companies for this sort of commerce, she would today have some powerful ones that would support themselves entirely at their own expense, instead of having only some isolated privileged persons who are incapable of moving their branches to distant places as fast as the Indian tribes move further away, and of commanding respect. Furthermore, the privileged persons collaborate with their foreign agents to defraud the sovereign, leaving to the treasury the responsiblity of political expenses that they had fully paid only in the first years of encouragement. They buy with long-term credits at second and third hand, and depend on the trade of the current year for the payment of their debts. And finally, because of the insufficiency of their wealth, they settle in places of habitation which are now too remote to realize from this commerce an overall profit, and they inspire a feeling of envy by an apparent affluence while not even gathering together enough means to dispose of their shipments during the regular seasons. Moreover, they are satisfied with that taste for a debauched and vagabond life which they acquire through exposure to the Indians, and remove themselves from the labors of a peaceful and fertile soil that would have enriched them long ago.

If, I say, Spain had favored and strictly supervised such companies for the benefit of the province, she would today have respectable business houses on the faraway banks of the Missouri. She would also be familiar with the headwaters of a river whose nearness to the Pacific Ocean would perhaps eventually be of great importance, and the commerce of the principal cities in the province of Louisiana would someday rival that of Canada. Carondelet, in whose favor I have always made an exception regarding corruptness and indifference in his administration, was well convinced, I am told, of that political importance. But, unfortunately, he arrived at a time when the feelings of the inhabitants had the effect of inspiring him with distrust, and his preference for companies to trade with the Indians resulted in a contract with foreigners.

I shall not elaborate any more on this matter, since I would end up repeating what I have already said about peltry in the course of my *Observations*. When I shall concern myself with the topography of the province, I shall have occasion to speak about it again, through the connections that fur trading has with Pensacola, the Illinois country, and other settlements.

CHAPTER SIX

Analytical Topography Based on Interrelationships Among Politics, Agriculture, and Commerce

In the descriptions that follow, I shall not limit them to the Spanish possessions on the Mississippi. I have always undertaken to examine the commercial and political aspects of this river in relation to the owners of its outlet to the Gulf; and whatever division or subdivision may be made of the territory through which the Mississippi or its branches flow, the province of Louisiana is always a single entity as regards its situation and prosperity, and is wholly dependent on the possession of the one port [New Orleans] that nature has given it for its exports. An impartial view of the Mississippi and its branches, navigable up to 800 or 900 leagues from its mouth and flowing along the most fertile lands of North America, will show that a population transplanted to its banks is all that Louisiana requires in order to enjoy riches, peace, and liberty. Half a million souls, prosperous in their first endeavors on the American side of the river and its branches, already guarantee by their experiences the success of settlements that could be encouraged in Louisiana where the lands are richer, more extensive, and easier to cultivate. The example of the east bank of the Mississippi, as well as public interest and politics, demonstrates the necessity to settle the west bank; but nothing has been done in that regard by the Spanish government, unless it was by Carondelet for whom the revolution hindered all initiatives. The original French inhabitants, who have not grown in numbers, are still in the same place where their government established them; some foreign families, hardly encouraged by the subordinate officials, have joined them there; and if positive information is available regarding the course and navigation of the rivers that have their sources in the west, it is due to the courage of hunters and enterprising traders, but not at all to the government's concern and encouragement.

I should make a comment about the map that I attach to my *Observations*. It is, as to the Mississippi, superior to any other map which has yet appeared; and as for the details which it contains, I am greatly obliged to Mr. Barthélemy Lafon, architect of New Orleans, who worked steadfastly to secure the information that he gave to me [see Map of the Mississippi and Its Branches].[1] The map that I offer here is based on his sketches which were copied in my presence. The territories through which I have passed while traveling have appeared to me to be quite accurately presented; and the omissions of topographical information, as will be seen in the outer boundaries of this map, are due to the impossibility of obtaining sketches during my travels.

It is inconceivable that, for the period of almost forty years the Spaniards have owned Louisiana, they have not at this time a properly constituted plan of their settlements in Upper and Lower Louisiana. The maps of the French surveyors and geographers, who had just been able to sketch only the borders of the Mississippi and the mouths of various rivers, are almost the only ones existing among the mass of papers in the Spanish secretariat, and are still the best ones to follow. It is only by the comparative reports of travelers and inhabitants that one comes to know some more instructive details in that regard. River banks, lakes, little streams, and the lands that have become or were always arable in all of the marshes that form Lower Louisiana, are only known to the hunters who frequent them, or else the government has only fragmented details which it never troubled to put together.

With this map before me, I am going to address myself to the topography of that immense territory, but some areas shall be mentioned only briefly, where it would be necessary for me to go and survey them myself in order to identify them with certainty since neither the government nor the colonists, I believe, know their description. After having attempted, as I have done through the course of my *Observations*, to prove that a bad political policy by the Spanish court and often a worse administration on the part of its representatives, had hampered the prosperity of Louisiana, I shall perhaps consider myself justified in embellishing on what its situation and its future promise. But I shall never be other than factual in connection with Louisiana's present condition, the qualities of its soil, and the inconveniences of its climate.

If, before entering the muddy approaches to the Mississippi, one takes note of the possessions on the Gulf of Mexico which Louisiana has under its control, there is first of all, the Floridas toward the east, known under the designation of East and West. East Florida, of no importance in its population and products, has on the ocean, at the northern mouth of the Bahama Channel, the port of St. Augustine which maintains, in fact, only a simple military relationship with Louisiana or even with Havana. Possession of that part of the territory surrounding the Gulf is doubtless necessary for the greatest security of the rest; but since it is so situated as neither to be able to establish commercial dealings with Louisiana nor to have any effect on its prosperity, it is omitted from the plan that I have proposed. If among its sands there are some lands capable of producing the same crops as in

89

Louisiana, it is probable that East Florida will require more expense for its protection, once it is well settled, than its agriculture could ever pay for. The Indians, whose hunting grounds are near St. Augustine, trade with that post; and the English business house, whose principal office is at Pensacola, maintains a branch there because of its preferential status.

Appalachicola Bay, into which the Appalachicola River flows, is located at the curve in the Gulf of Mexico where the shore of West Florida commences. On that bay, admirably situated for trading with some of the Indian tribes now known by the name of Creeks, the government maintains a fort [St. Marks] with a garrison, having no purpose except to protect one of the branches of that privileged business firm of Pensacola. It is there that Bowles—of whom I have had occasion to speak in the course of my observations on government, and who was the sworn enemy of that business firm by which he had once been arrested—several years ago [1792] came to carry out his sudden attack, perhaps seeking more to satisfy his personal vengeance than to attend to the business or political projects which had been confided to him. I have already said enough about his misfortunes and some fleeting successes which he later realized, but what I should again mention is that he continues to harass the Spaniards; that he has already cost them more than 150,000 piastres, and threatening in turn St. Augustine, the Appalachicola Bay area, and even Pensacola, he deprives New Orleans of a large part of its garrison. In fact, he gives proof of the Spanish government's weakness, and the meager influence and position which it has been able to maintain for itself among the Indians. Fortunately, the privileged business firm at Pensacola gained more for itself than he did, otherwise Bowles would have been able to have a far greater number of Indians revolt.

There are no settlements in that area other than the fort, and no population other than the little garrison that it needs. Nearby there is a quarry of excellent stone, and the lands are,

as in general throughout Florida, either low or cut up by
many streams, sandy, covered with pine trees, and not at all
adaptable for settlement except on the lake shores and river
banks. If it were possible to form them into a league against
the Spaniards, the Indians could still gather together 10,000
to 12,000 warriors, not including the Cherokees, who trade
more directly with the state of Tennessee or other United
States inhabitants living near them west of the Appalachians.

In following the coast of West Florida westward, one comes
to the port of Pensacola, sheltered, as is its bay, by Santa Rosa
Island. This place in not only important because of the
considerable trade still carried on with the Chickasaw, Choc-
taw, and Creek Indians—among whom are some of the tribes
called *Alabamond* and *Talapouches* by the French, and who are
generally known as Upper and Lower Creeks—but it is also
of very great political significance. Pensacola is the only port
that can provide a harbor for government vessels, especially
in wartime, when the mother country of Louisiana, con-
voying its supplies and exports, will see that her flag is
respected in the Gulf of Mexico and will not permit a common privateer from New Providence to control the mouth of
the Mississippi. The English, under whom every colony
prospers, had already made Pensacola an important post.
When it was taken from them in the war [1781] prior to the
last one, the barracks, the port, and the fortifications had that
stability and solidarity which they know how to give to their
possessions. And if at the time England did not have complete ownership of Louisiana, the commerce in which she had
begun to participate was sufficient to make her provide for
herself a safe and convenient port on the Gulf of Mexico.
Moreover, she was assured an additional storage place for
that contraband trade which she carries on within the
Spanish possessions in the New World, and which transfers
into her hands the greater portion of the net profits realized
by working the Spanish mines.

Why, if everything prospers under the control of an Eng-

91

lishman, does it all disintegrate under that of the Spaniards? Pensacola is now nothing but a hovel, where the garrison can no longer be housed; the military and civil buildings are in ruins, and if there has been any work in connection with the local fortifications or repairs to several disabled ships or frigates, the slowness and indifference which the Spaniards have brought to those tasks have proven that they never undertake them for the glory and welfare of the state. An English frigate, often even some privateer from New Providence, frequently pillaged the settlements along the shore and effectively interrupted the vital coastal shipping between Pensacola and New Orleans. Nor would the English have been averse to destroying Pensacola if their government had thought that Spain could gain a political advantage through it, and if the business profits made had not been passed on to them, since a London firm has a monopoly there.

Pensacola is the headquarters of the privileged business firm of W. Panton and Company. It is there that ships coming from England bring supplies for the Indian trade, and on the return voyage they take with them the pelts which they exclusively handle. It is there, in fact, that the various agencies and warehouses on the rivers and among the Indian tribes receive their orders and supplies. Of course, the widespread branches of that important firm—which for a long time has established across the country a mail service with the United States at its own expense, so that it would lack nothing to assure its business affairs and prosperity—might serve as an example to the Spanish government for encouraging the means of making a direct profit out of the other Indian trading areas. The Spanish court probably has not concerned itself with the danger—any more than it would have seen the injustice—of enriching and placing in authority in its territory by such a monopoly, strangers with whom it is often at war, and against whom it had only recently conquered the community to which the monopoly extends.[2]

Spain certainly compensated herself to release Panton and Company from the financial shackles of the province of Louisiana. But how is it that she did not inquire as to the results, so as to found, on a more solid and more advantageous base, the Indian trade along the Mississippi and its branches? What a pitiful contrast between Panton's privileges and those given to men of moderate means, and the limited Indian trade which others would like to obtain. Where are their numerous warehouses and workshops for the labor which the handling of pelts requires? Where are the ships which bring them directly all the articles of Indian trade, and which, loading pelts in the regular season for the account of traders with exclusive privileges, assure the success of that branch of commerce to the advantage of the province? Finally, where is the assurance of moral and political influence that traders similar to Panton will obtain among the Indians to repulse the competition and encroachments of the enemy? There are none, and on the contrary one will find in such Indian trade all the disadvantages which I have previously mentioned. The designation of exclusive privilege carries with it something odious; but politically and morally speaking, in the situation in which Louisiana finds itself, some wealthy company, treated preferentially but scrupulously supervised, ought to be established for the Indian trade, as it is proven that annual contracts to supply the Indians are indispensable to support them and to keep them in line.

The Panton firm, besides its correspondent in London and several others in various places, had one in the colony of New Providence, whose piracy has continually devastated the commerce of New Orleans. That circumstance often encouraged patriotic envy and hatred toward Mr. Panton. To slander him they accused him of espionage and of informing the pirate shipowners with whom, they said, he was associated. But if such a charge is ever made, I deny it in advance with much pleasure which I express by a plea of fairness and gratitude toward an honorable and beneficient business house, under whose protection all unfortunates will find help and consolation. Shipwrecks have often brought their victims to Pensacola, as I was myself in 1796; and without distinction of rank, nationality, and belief, all receive a most generous hospitality. To the great regret of the commerce of New Orleans, that firm still enjoys a trade which enriches it and, like others, it surely will have profited from the vacillating policies of the Spanish government to give all possible expansion to its monopoly. But who would not have done the same?

It could be said that Pensacola is maintained only for the convenience of the Panton firm, since, for the local residents, agriculture and commerce are nonexistent there and, with the Spanish fleet rotting in the port of Havana instead of protecting shipping in the Gulf, that harbor is of no use to them. The headquarters staff of the military post, the garrison of one battalion, the Panton firm, some tavern keepers and tradesmen, several makers of earthenware, and perhaps 300 slaves, buy from New Orleans only foodstuffs and liquors, and in return sell some quicklime, bricks, tiles, paving stones, pots and molds, and yellow and violet clay with which both the rich and poor colonists often paint the rooms of their living quarters. The pine forests can also provide rosin and tar, but the opening up of markets for all these products is dependent entirely upon the demands of commerce in New Orleans, which obtains some of them much nearer at hand.

Pensacola is built almost entirely on sand at the beginning of a broad stretch of land of the same material which extends in a larger expanse as far as Mobile Bay. The soil in the Floridas offers nothing of exceptional quality. But when the wealth of Louisiana will have demonstrated the vital need for the port of Pensacola, they will find there, in addition to the importance of materials available on the spot to revive its settlements, a healthfulness more highly esteemed than any other location in Lower Louisiana could offer—for slaves, ships' companies, and additional garrisons for military service. The forests of the Mississippi River will supply stocks of lumber and masts of all kinds. Fort Pitt, the Illinois and Ouachita regions, and the Kentucky settlements, will provide iron, hemp, lead, and copper, whether ore or manufactured. And if France, in fact, regained its former possessions on the Gulf of Mexico, that port, so indispensable for the security of Louisiana, could add to its political importance the warehousing of a considerable trade, either contraband or by agreement between France and the United States, so long as Spain does not become a more industrial nation.

A careful examination of the map [Map of the Mississippi and Its Branches] will show convincingly the safety and ease of communication between Pensacola and New Orleans. The only section normally exposed to the perils of war and bad weather is the coast between New Orleans and Mobile Bay, but communication there can be effected only in ships of thirty to forty tons burden. Even then, navigation becomes difficult at the approaches to New Orleans. When I describe that capital, I shall indicate the reasons for the navigational hazards. Now I shall proceed with the details, as concisely as possible, which I think should be given regarding the portion of the Gulf which concerns Louisiana.

At about fifteen leagues west of Pensacola, a chain of islands begins, protecting different bays and river mouths at which the French founded their first settlements at the time of their initial attempts at colonization in Louisiana. Following that chain of islands, one arrives at the outlet of the lakes forming the northern boundary of Lower Louisiana, whose opposite shore, in a continuation of the elevation and quality of the land, extends the Floridas to the post of Baton Rouge on the Mississippi.[3] The extent of this ridge varies along the waterways, as it does around the lakes and the Gulf, and winds its way, often higher in elevation along the left bank of the Mississippi as far as the mouth of the Ohio. The ridge then goes on to join with a chain of mountains that border, in turning toward the south, the left bank of the Tennessee for about fifty leagues, and finally resumes for a longer distance on the same bank of the Tennessee toward the east, the slight elevation that it has along the shores of the Gulf. The lands of West Florida, from the high ground on the left bank of the Mississippi up to the mouth of the Ohio, and from those lands in the central region occupied by the Indians—all contained within the contour of the ridge that I have just described—are, with few exceptions, of very inferior quality and often quite bad. The banks of the rivers near their mouths—along the outline that I have just traced —afford some land and opportunity for fairly good settlements, but in general it is an extensive area of very sandy soil, more or less intersected by hills, and bordered to the east by the settlements of the United States behind Charleston and Savannah, and to the south by some pine forests, swamps, virgin prairies, and mounds of sand. To the west there is often a ridge, higher, less sandy, but more eroded by the depth of its slopes; then some extensive marshes called cypress swamps because of the many cypress trees found in them. To the north there are some steep mountains near the mouth of the Tennessee, and some less arid land upstream of that river; and finally, at the center, a sandy interior covered with oaks and stunted walnut trees. In the slopes of those mountains arise the streams which eventually, after much meandering, flow into the Tennessee, the Mississippi, the lakes, and the Gulf of Mexico. When describing the settlements along the left bank of the Mississippi, I shall mention some exceptions to the above outline, and I now return to the southern borders of those lands.

The Spaniards have a post with some settlers stationed at Mobile Bay, as much for the protection of trading with the Choctaws, Chickasaws, and other Indians, under the privileged firm at Pensacola, as for the safety of the very small population located there. It was on that bay and the one at Pascagoula that the French established themselves in 1699 and 1702; but if they soon recognized the superiority of the lands in Lower Louisiana, they also saw the need to abandon settlements having no natural protection, so as to relocate where nature defended them against attack. Accordingly, they left first Biloxi and then Mobile Bay, and came, about 1717, to found New Orleans. Nevertheless, all the rivers sheltered and protected by the sand islands could some day provide an increase in agriculture and commerce, just as those which flow into the lakes of Lower Louisiana and which, better protected by their location, already enjoy a glimmer of prosperity.[4] Numerous herds of cattle are raised there, and rosin and tar, quicklime, and vegetable wax are produced also. Some trapping is carried on. Cotton might be cultivated successfully; and some timber cut, of which the ease of exploitation would compensate for the better quality of the timber along the Mississippi. In order for that to happen it would be necessary for the colonists to be encouraged and supported in peacetime, and, during hostilities, that a fortified town at Pensacola and a naval force in the Gulf not abandon the poor inhabitants and their shipping to the mercy of New Providence's pirates.

Leaving the chain of islands that runs from east to west, and turning south toward the mouth of the Mississippi, one arrives at Round Bay [Breton Sound] into which the streams emptying into that river occasionally overflow. It is always necessary to wait there, quite anxiously and often dangerously, for a wind to make it possible to reach the entrance to the river's passes. To the west of these passes there are other bays in which changeable currents can alter a ship's direction, the most dangerous being St. Bernard Bay [Galveston Bay] which recalls many unfortunate incidents. Its history might have been embellished, but certainly the Indians, of whom several tribes still inhabit its shores—whether or not they are cannibals—have murdered many victims whom ignorance or the irresistible force of the currents brought there. Trinity River—sighted by De La Salle in 1685, at the headwaters of which his own companions made him suffer the fate from which he had escaped at the hands of the Indians—flows into that bay; and now that the province of Texas is becoming populated and growing rapidly, there is reason to hope that commerce and civilization will soon bring fresh life to places which ignorance and ferocity stained with blood.

From St. Bernard Bay to the mouth of the Mississippi specific details of the coast are not known, even though it borders the most fertile lands of Lower Louisiana. Maps of the interior also are not available, despite the fact that prosperity, as prompt as it is assured, for the Opelousas and Attakapas posts might be the result of a direct route which would supply them and provide a market for their products. I shall talk at greater length later about these settlements, and I return now to the passes of the Mississippi.

I am not aware of, nor does my map [Map of a Portion of Lower Louisiana and Western Florida] indicate, the practical or theoretical means of approaching the passes of the Mississippi River, or the easiest way of going through them; but I might point out that as the narrow ship channels often change, it would be foolhardy to rely on a hydographic survey however recent or thorough in its details.[5] Some mud flats at sea level, covered with bulrush five to six feet high (shown on this map without small dots), are the only bearings that nature provides on that shore. The old French lighthouse, sunk in the mud or destroyed by shifting of the passes, has been replaced by the Spaniards at the point indicated, on a clearing along one of the river's passes, which, in what is mapped of its course, has a depth of fifteen or twenty feet of water and then loses itself in the sands. The East Pass, where this lighthouse or beacon is located, is the one most frequently used because it continually has the greatest depth, thereby avoiding the costs of lightering and reloading, although generally it does not take ships drawing more than fourteen feet. The West Pass is the next most frequented, particularly by ships whose destination is that part of the Gulf of Mexico, and offering the advantage in wartime of being able to enter or leave in spite of enemy vessels which circumstances have brought and kept to the east of the river's mouth. The South Pass is not used because of the mud which has obstructed it more and more, and, finally, the Northeast Pass and Pass à Loutre can be used only by ships drawing no more than nine feet of water.

In order to build the small lighthouse at Balise, the Spaniards erected a levee with earth fill which, extended a distance of 400 to 500 feet, serves as a foundation for the huts necessary to house several soldiers, a customs agent, and some river pilots. Perhaps it would have been more advantageous to place these buildings at the upper end of the passes, but what is certain is that the pilots, all Spaniards by birth, and I venture to say by character, are as slow as they are careless in performing their duties. They hardly condescend to go outside the sandbars to work the ships, although there is perhaps no place in the world where it would be more necessary for them to go far out to meet the ships and to help them avoid the contrary winds, currents, and tides in the bays east and west of the Mississippi. The flow of the current of the river into the Gulf would favor the pilot's labors in that respect, and they then would earn the twenty piastres gourdes allotted to them; but no, they confine themselves to the part where a pilot is required to go—the tenth of a mile beyond the sandbars! After that, any careful ship captain going up to New Orleans can do without a river pilot.

Ascending the river from the Balise to New Orleans, about eleven leagues upriver, at the first sharp bend which the Mississippi forms, there is a fort maintained by the Spaniards, with a garrison eaten up by the insects from the desolate and uncultivable swamps surrounding it.⁶ Several leagues beyond this fort, that adds nothing to the obstacles which nature itself provides against an invasion, there begin some miserable settlements which, too scattered to provide protection for each other, fall victim to floods and show their effects. It was in this very area that the first attempt at colonization took place, before moving up to the vicinity where New Orleans is located.⁷ But today as far up as English Turn there is only a sparse population, few plantations of much value, and only one on the left bank, well known because of the generous hospitality of its owner, Monsieur de Gentilly, who has sixty to eighty Negro slaves.⁸ However, this part of the river might one day be more productive, but that will only happen with the aid of the government when, stirring itself to facilitate communications and to improve navigation, it initiates projects which the importance of the area would soon make indispensable. Already the government's solicitude should have been awakened in that regard by the part of the Mississippi known as English Turn, which, because of the variety of winds needed to navigate it by sail, and because of the diffficulty of towing, often delays very important shipping operations, increases their eventual expenses and causes all these inconveniences to reflect upon the prosperity of the colony. This improvement by the government would also enhance the value of arable lands below English Turn by providing incentives for their cultivation. While these lands are generally too low for cotton, sugar, and indigo, and thus cannot add to the production of those commodities, they would lend themselves to the cultivation of rice and corn, provide naval stores already so often unavailable at the port of New Orleans, and increase the number of sawmills cutting the cypress trees from the swamps.

From the far end of the bend in the river at English Turn, for about four leagues, both banks are well populated up to New Orleans. Ten sugarhouses and almost as many sawmills give an important value to that area. For those plantations (as well as those of the other settlements in Lower Louisiana) to become extensive properties, only slaves are lacking, the importation of which the colonists themselves prevented in a moment of fear and which the mother country now impedes by the meaningless monopolies which she grants in Europe.

At the far end of the bend at English Turn, which I referred to above, a little stream opens out toward the east, whose high banks have served as a refuge for emigrants from the Canary Islands, who are known here as Islanders. That area is called *La Terre aux Boeufs*, and this new settlement transplanted there around 1783, languished a long time under the illusory benefits which the government gave them. But now, either by supplying food for the city or by cooperating among themselves to make sugar, they live in easier circumstances; and their limited attempts at growing cotton promise more success in the future than that commodity offers for lands on the banks of the river extending from the second parish *des Allemands* to its mouth.[9] The population of *La Terre aux Boeufs* consists of not more than one hundred families, including several Acadian families; all settled along the banks of its bayou, or little river, emptying into Lake Borgne some leagues away. But they will be able to expand this settlement when they so desire, for around the edge of Lake Borgne are a number of other bayous whose banks are high, and several large areas surrounded by oak trees [*chênières*] where dairy farms have been established.[10]

This description of the nature and condition of lands along the Mississippi prompts me, before I go into further details, to give a general view of the land of Lower Louisiana through which the Mississippi flows. By a peculiarity perhaps unique, the highest places in all these lands are the banks of the Mississippi and of the bayous, as well as the shores of the lakes. This high ground provides the only means they have of establishing plantations; and it generally consists of good soil, rarely with too much clay in it, more often loamy with an adequate mixture of sand, varying considerably in depth, and only in certain circumstances connecting with the high ground along another lake or river. Because of this unique situation, concessions of land are granted in arpents measured fronting on the waterways and going back as far as possible to the muddy lands at the rear, which serve as drainage for the higher ground. These low areas receive, during spring floods, rainwater and seepage water from crevasses caused by the weather and poor maintenance of levees, as well as the water used for irrigation and operation of the sawmills. Thus, one can say that in Louisiana surface water does not drain to the streams. Unfortunately, it follows from that fact, that in the area located north of the Mississippi (that is, the area bounded by the Mississippi's left bank, the right bank of the Iberville, Lakes Maurepas, Pontchartrain, and Borgne, and the shores of Round Bay), and in the area south of the Mississippi (that is, the area from the Atchafalaya, between the right bank of the Mississippi and the left banks of the various bayous and lakes, to the shores of Barataria Bay), there is a mass of stagnant water which during several months of the year produces a putrid odor from the dangerous mires in which it has collected.

To the planter's greatest advantage, arable land fortunately extends quite a distance along both banks of the river to the rear; however, this depth can vary from a fraction of an arpent to thirty ordinarily, rarely as much as sixty, and in unusual cases up to one hundred arpents.[11] The lands bordering the lakes, being generally narrower, are consequently closer to the muddy areas, and there are connections among the lakes through the opening of the bayous which carry out part of the water. Scattered throughout this section are cypress forests, oak trees, and virgin prairies. In order to reach a decision with respect to filling in the low places, drying and improving them—many of which undoubtedly are susceptible to such improvement—it would be necessary to have surveys and measurements made by competent individuals, and to be inspired by a desire to make a colony prosper in a way that the Spanish government has not yet evidenced.

This surface condition of Lower Louisiana gives it a disagreeable aspect, isolates the planters, and makes it difficult for them to travel around. It is an immense swamp that must be studied for a long time before it can be crossed without danger; and necessity alone could induce pioneer colonists to settle in such places that nature apparently has destined ony as a refuge for crocodiles, snakes, and a million species of insects which still seem to claim its ownership.

It would be wrong to assume from this summary that Lower Louisiana is an unhealthy country. To assume so would be to take a part for the whole in applying that judgment throughout its area, since it is only New Orleans that for some years has suffered epidemics. This is perhaps the result of local conditions the details of which I shall discuss presently; but it is certain that the planters who are compelled by the nature of the soil to adapt themselves to narrow strips of land not so low as New Orleans, in no way suffer from the effects of the climate. Moreover, the afflictions to which a stranger is exposed when reaching Louisiana are, in general, never so deadly as in the colonies throughout the tropics.

The banks of the Mississippi to which I have just referred, and where the principal plantations are still located, can be cultivated only by the presence of levees that prevent them from being flooded during high water. These levees, built for the benefit of individuals as well as the general public, should be a matter of concern to the government, as much for extending them along the river as for their upkeep and rebuilding. But, as I think I've already mentioned, and perhaps because their necessary maintenance returns no profit, they are abandoned to the most culpable neglect. The planter, sole master of his labors in that regard, undertakes his dilatory repairs only at the most threatening places. In its overflows, this, one of the largest rivers in the world, often has less resistance to overcome than is offered to the smallest streams in other countries. As a consequence, every year in the bends of the river crevasses occur that first lay waste the immediately adjacent crops, then inundate the low backlands, and recede finally to their banks, devastating other planters as well as those primarily responsible for the crevass. To avoid these frequent disasters one could hardly take enough precautions, and some supervisory officials—such as for filling in, draining, and so on—ought to provide the basis of regulations which, not abandoning the inhabitant to his own efforts, might indicate to him when and where to use his labor to prevent crevasses, and, especially, the caving in of levees. Thus individual interest could be balanced against the general welfare. The roads and bridges, as well as shipping on navigable bayous, are also neglected. Spain may have some excellent regulations in that regard, but they are most often silent on a subject which involves the welfare of the planter, ease of communication, and the colony's health.

I am now going to continue my *Observations* in detail, which I had interrupted above at the gates of New Orleans. When resources for the colonists in the entire province were available only in the settlements of Lower Louisiana, which the government had no desire at all to increase, it is not surprising that New Orleans was regarded as a miserable port condemned to the paltry exportation of products from the swamps which surrounded it. Under such circumstances, it would have taken many centuries to bring it to the point where it is today, but now that 400,000 to 500,000 souls live at the sources of the Mississippi's tributaries, what statesman could view the situation of New Orleans without imagining that it must one day be very prosperous? Located near the mouth of a river whose waters dominate a territory almost as vast as all Europe, one's imagination can run wild, without exaggeration, in thinking about the good fortune which the present and the immediate future promises New Orleans, without deluding one's self too much. By its commanding position in this vast country, New Orleans will assemble in its port a huge amount of commodities from the Torrid Zones for exportation along with products from the Temperate Zones. It will offer the most advantageous assortment of goods for European and West Indian cargoes. It can, in fact, expect to become one of the richest markets of the New World. The future alone can vindicate me in that respect; and before I give a short description of New Orleans, the condition in which I found it in 1796 should be recalled, when Kentucky and other settlements had not yet had any influence whatever on its commerce. One should also make a comparison of the results at this time of that same commerce and finally, calculate what a European power, whose politics induce it to take the necessary measures, could do to make Louisiana prosper.

New Orleans, situated about 29° 07′ latitude and 92° 20′ longitude, rises on the banks of a bend or crescent in the left bank of the Mississippi, and comprises within its fortifications a square half a mile long on the bend [*quarré*], a little over a quarter of a mile wide.[12] A strong levee protects it from floods on the river side; and evenly intersected by ten streets of about 40 feet in width from the southeast to the northwest, and five cross streets from the southwest to the northeast, it is divided into islets of approximately 250 feet frontage on each side, and then in a parallel line at the front of the city whose point nearest to the river is like a tangent to the deepest part of its bend.[13] The only public square reserved for its enjoyment is at the center of the city's river front; for the empty spaces in the angles formed by the river at the southeast and southwest corners of the city, designed to serve as parade grounds for the forts, cannot be called public squares.[14]

The fortifications of New Orleans consist of three stockades enclosing the city on all sides except the river front, and four small forts with embankments, of little value, one at each far corner of the city, and capable of firing their guns toward the interior as well as the exterior. They were rather intended to serve as a refuge for the friends of the government in case of an insurrection, so dreaded from 1793 to 1796, than to guard against an enemy attempting to capture the city.[15] Midway on each of the long stockades that connect the four forts, there is a battery on a projecting angle. A ditch about twenty feet wide and four feet deep, with no connection to those of the forts, and without a protected or banked roadway, surrounds the city and completes its defenses. These fortifications have been quite neglected, although there was a period when, because of fright and anxiety, much time, money, and labor were devoted to them. But, actually forts are not necessary at New Orleans; the difficulty of navigation and the dangers from its swamps protect it from all invasions. If there exist, more or less distant from the city, some places where one could land in Lower Louisiana, that is where it will be necessary some day to establish a close watch; they would be modern-day Passes of Thermopylae, where a hundred well-trained men could victoriously repulse the attacks of several thousands. It is there, of course, that redoubts or forts would be indispensable to the security of the province; for if an enemy were interested in properly arming itself, and in being guided by night up to the eastern stockades of New Orleans, it would very soon have convinced the government of the uselessness of its fortifications.

Although when referring to the police I have mentioned the military forces of the colony, I think I should mention that the garrison of New Orleans consists specifically of the Louisiana Regiment's First Battalion (except for the withdrawals which the official duties of the province require), the Second Battalion being at Pensacola for service in East and West Florida; a Second Battalion of the Mexican Regiment more precisely attached to duty in the *Place d'Armes;* a head-quarters staff, and several artillerymen; a company of dragoons; two engineers and several officers from river vessels. The governor general, deprived of a post comman-dant, aided by a post-adjutant and two staff officers, directs, as I have mentioned, the civil and military services even to the most minute details. Around this continually active force, there gathers a crowd of officers, nearly all useless, of an undisciplined militia, many of whom are not attached to any company, or never join it at its headquarters, or have even obtained a commission only to avoid all military duty! That abuse can, on occasion, become even more harmful to the colony; since the naturally brave Creoles, alert and very skillful, by reason of the locality could organize a militia which troops recruited elsewhere would never equal in effectiveness.

Beyond its limits, New Orleans now also has a suburb properly subdivided for development, equal at least to its length and half as wide extending upriver to the southwest.[16] To the east, downstream, it has fields so close together that their frontage forms, so to speak, a second suburb.[17] And finally, to the north there is its third outlet, known as Bayou Road, where little houses are so near to one another they could soon also form a new suburb. All of those areas are quite far from being densely populated; but the frontages along the river or on the road alone provide a large part of the total area that would be needed for the entire city where 100,000 souls could then be settled, while now they total at least 10,000, of which not less than half are white and the remainder slaves and free people of color.

Two disastrous conflagrations, in 1788 and 1794, all the more serious each time in burning a third of the town, reduced in size a few large fortunes while eliminating a vast number of moderate ones, which prosperity can eventually restore but not always put back into the same hands. New

Orleans, a town largely of frame construction, had rebuilt with the same material after the calamitous fire of 1788; but experience and more prosperous circumstances led to the replacement of the traces of the 1794 conflagration with brick buildings. Half of the destroyed structures are already safely and solidly rebuilt, and the quantity of existing large and commodious commercial buildings foreshadows prosperous times. New Orleans has 1,000 to 1,200 buildings, of which 700 to 800 houses are still of frame construction, in poor condition and very old, where the owner or occupant awaits, with a kind of resignation, another conflagration. Such a disaster, always dreaded and always alarming in its terrible effects, could someday, if one were forewarned, become a sort of benefit in that part of New Orleans, for the buildings there are deteriorating rapidly from lack of care, because of an ordinance that prohibits repairs to the roofs of old houses with other than tile, slate, or flagstone, and they cost more to demolish than they are worth. There are mostly shanties along the blocks of the third [Bourbon] street parallel to the river front, and indeed fence posts are often the only indication of building sites. It will be a long time before building construction is undertaken there, even when an active commerce will have established a larger population in the city that requires immense storehouses, unless meanwhile an ordinance inhibits suburban growth, and a government concerns itself with drainage, improvements, and betterments which would be beneficial to that area.

New Orleans can provide a safe harbor for an unlimited number of ships, and facilities to discharge and to load more than fifty at a time. The city is still under obligation to the French for most of its public buildings and those used by representatives of the king. Government House, the barracks, storehouses, are still such as the French built them; and if it has a church, a city hall, and a charity hospital, New Orleans owes these estimable institutions to the superstition of a parvenu Spaniard who covered himself with blessings and honor by this means.[18] The municipal officers, known as the *cabildo* and their assistants, are absolutely useless, as I have already said and should repeat, in the maintenance of discipline and security, because of the domineering influence that the governor general takes toward them.[19]

In the overall view that I have given of security in the colony, I made abundantly clear the circumstances which were able to affect New Orleans. I have also talked about its judiciary that, lacking a courtroom, practices its corruption with impunity in the shadows; but those two subjects are turbid waters that, in order to avoid contaminating my readers, I no longer want to stir up.[20] The customhouse, crudely built of wood, has in its structure, through a sense of justice I believe, the appearance of a workhouse for convicts and I shall not undertake to defile my pen again with an account of their thefts and depravities. Finally, the treasury that believes it is contributing to the happiness of the colony because it reluctantly lets gold circulate, has its offices and coffers in a rented house, and spreads as much as possible its barren and sterile ideas.

I shall say nothing more about the religion of this city; the tolerance of its clergymen presents an incredible contrast with their severity and influence in other Spanish colonies. Generally speaking, the believer, while alive, is never apprehensive, provided he makes his confession before dying and his descendants can imitate him in peace, however negligent they may be in the performance of their own religious duties. New Orleans has a bishop, a number of canons, a parish priest, some curates, and several other secular clergymen or monks, but there is neither a bishopric, nor rectory, nor a monastery for men. There is a convent for nuns for which the town is also indebted to the French, and it is there that many young ladies go to improve their Christian education in a complete absence of worldly instruction. The Spaniards, for the benefit of the boys, have endowed an Ignorantine brother who teaches reading and writing to the extent he knows, and explains as he can the sacred mysteries.[21] Beyond that, the solicitude of the government has done nothing to provide public facilities for education.

The climate and healthfulness of New Orleans call for some particular observations. In the latitude where it is located, it ought to enjoy the advantages of a moderate climate, which indeed in many respects it does. Autumn and spring there are quite agreeable; winter is often mild, and if a stranger, sometimes even a colonist, becomes the victim of a pestilential fever that manifests itself in a most violent way during the months of July, August, September, and October, it is the result of the combined neglect of the prevailing administrative regulations. In the course of my *Observations*, I have already indicated the principal causes: clogged drains; pools of stagnant and fetid water in all sections of town and in the gutters of all the sidewalks, as well as in the surrounding country where they are the result of receding crevasses; garbage and dead animals lying all over the streets; burials of strangers made without supervision, and those of Roman Catholics too close together for the nature of the soil; the poor quality of meat products, when a widely extended supervision could secure a better grade, and the pestilential filthy places where they are sold; the great distress that gives an epidemic character to diseases for which there is only an illusory refuge in a charity hospital, previously mentioned, whose arrangement and means limit its care of the sick; and finally, there are all the measures taken by a government, unconcerned about every kind of improvement, that seem to accentuate the deficiencies of a swampland which, perhaps, without those measures, would enjoy in certain places, as it did in the past, all the healthfulness of a salubrious soil.

Lower Louisiana, it is true, in the absence of a steady

breeze, experiences some hot weather as intense as that in the tropics, but if its filth and stench caused some diseases, why are they concentrated within the limits of New Orleans? Why is it that outside the city, in all the areas of Lower Louisiana, they do not suffer from those deadly fevers that persist in killing foreigners, and from which they and the colonists perish only when their business requires them to be in New Orleans? Why is it only in that city that every two or three years germs and contagion manifest themselves, and why are diseases never more mortal than during the years when crevasses have saturated the cemeteries and covered the outskirts of the town with decayed debris of animals and vegetables? No, Lower Louisiana is not an unhealthy place. Only in its city is centered the pollution that tears it down. An active government, benevolent and enlightened, would have soon eliminated it; and surveys, landfills, and, of course, drainage, would generally provide in healthfulness of the area compensation for what other colonial countries freely provide under similar conditions.

In the direction of one of the streets in the center of the town, from southeast to northwest, beyond its fortifications, New Orleans has a canal which connects with Bayou St. John and leads to its northern outlet, which bayou meanders east and west in traversing some of those exposed ridges suitable for settlement.[22] One of those lies to the east along Bayou Gentilly, whose arable lands join up with those at the far end of Lake Borgne; while the other, to the west, after having crossed Bayou St. John, makes accessible the whole length of Bayou Metairie where, as on the preceding one, there are several settlements. The canal about which I want to speak is a benefit from Carondelet's administration: it facilitates a highly useful communication with Pensacola, Mobile, the lakes, and their settlements. Before it was opened, the ships of that waterway docked about two miles from the city on Bayou St. John, while now they come into a basin at the foot of the fortifications to discharge their goods and load cargoes for the return voyage. If this improvement had been kept up, it would provide great encouragement to the planters of West Florida; but soon through culpable indifference and neglect of maintenance the choked and ruined canal will no longer be navigable. It needed, as a follow up to the arrangement made by Carondelet to open it, the cleaning out of Bayou St. John as far as Lake Pontchartrain, and the maintenance at its mouth of a pass as deep as possible. Perhaps, they might even consider giving to that project all the favorable extension to which it is susceptible, in opening the end of that canal at the basin and continuing it around the fortifications of the town as far as the Mississippi, but they have done nothing in that respect.[23] If the canal is filled with its own rubbish, the bayou is more and more blocked by debris and old trees that have fallen from its banks, and at normal tides pirogues can hardly go through its pass.

That is all I wanted to add to my remarks regarding the administration of New Orleans, whose good or bad results reflect on the well-being or adversity of the entire province. And in summarizing what I have previously said about the government of Louisiana in general, its finances, its judiciary, and so on, one will no longer be surprised if the wealth of Spain has for so long a time produced only discouragement, misery, or mediocrity there; if the waterways and communications have been blocked and the agricultural and commercial establishments in the colony have hardly supported themselves; and, finally, if New Orleans periodically becomes the grave of most foreigners who seek to establish themselves there.

Let us now leave New Orleans and go up the Mississippi River along both banks from New Orleans to the thirty-first parallel, which serves as the boundary between the territory of the United States and Lower Louisiana on the left bank. On both sides of the river are some settlements, quite close to one another, known as Tchoupitoulas, First and Second Parishes of the German Coast, parish of Cantrelle, parish of La Fourche, parishes of Manchac, Baton Rouge, Pointe Coupée, and, finally, Bayous *des Ecores*, Feliciana [Thompson's Creek], Torrika [Tunica], and Sara.[24] Behind the marshes and cypress groves of the left bank, on the southern shores of Lake Pontchartrain and Lake Maurepas, which are frequented only by hunters, there are no settlements. It is only at their headwaters behind Baton Rouge on the highlands that there is a community called Galveston along the Amite River.[25] There are none on the right bank of the Mississippi in whose low lands are the lakes and bayou of Barataria, noted for the quantity of duck and wild geese killed there every winter, that attracts a group of men who devote all their time to hunting, which is detrimental to agricultural pursuits and even more harmful to the health of those who engage in it. Those lakes have become considerably filled with debris since their discovery, and along their shores as on the banks of bayous, there are prairielands and woodlands where arrangements could be made to establish many settlements.

Near the shores of the Gulf of Mexico are several permanently located families, Acadians or from among those who now live at *Terre aux Boeufs*, all that is left of a much larger number who immigrated to that location. Their miserable existence is supported mainly by fishing, especially in gathering oysters, which they bring to town. And that area of lakes, bayous, oak trees, prairies, cypress groves, canes or reeds, mud flats, or hazardous places—so close to New Orleans—is still known in detail only by hunters. Then, on the right bank of the Mississippi are Bayou Lafourche and Bayou Plaquemines, about which I shall have to speak in the greatest detail, and all the more interesting because they lead beyond those low lands to the most important posts of

Lower Louisiana: Attakapas and Opelousas. Finally, above Pointe Coupée, there is the Atchafalaya River, which has its source at the Mississippi, and which requires particular observations that concern the physical and political existence of Lower Louisiana.

I have summarized, in my observations on commerce and agriculture, the total production along the Mississippi for the year 1801, and I shall not give the precise details by settlements because to secure them would have caused a further delay in writing these *Observations*. I shall be content to observe, for the satisfaction of the reader and to enable him to make an approximate calculation if an increase in population necessitated it, that of those settlements which I shall indicate, or which I have already mentioned for agriculture in Lower Louisiana, a total of about 10,000 to 12,000 laborers gathered the harvest of 1801, of which 4,000 at the most, on about sixty sugar plantations, made five to six million pounds of sugar. The other laborers picked or ginned almost six million pounds of cotton and furnished supplies of vegetables and livestock for the town, also supplies of rice, corn, and the small amount of indigo, tar, and pitch which they would have produced in that same year.

All of the districts between the thirtieth and thirty-first parallel, which I have just mentioned and whose specific description I am about to commence, extend for sixty leagues along the banks of the winding Mississippi, have the largest number of slaves, and consequently provide altogether the largest share of the current wealth in the Spanish possessions of Louisiana. Their population together with that of the city and its surrounding areas already described include at least four-fifths of the blacks, all of the free people of color, and more than half of the whites; that is to say, in fact, 40,000 to 45,000 individuals of all classes in Spanish subjects only, for I do not include in this estimate those of Natchez, who from force of habit are sometimes added.

The districts of Tchoupitoulas and the First German Parish, inhabited by about 3,500 blacks and 1,500 whites, have on both sides of the river the largest number of sugar plantations established in the province, primarily because their soil is most suitable, and the quantity of slaves, usually sufficient in number, has encouraged that cultivation. For several years nearly all the inhabitants have made their living from sugarcane, either in grinding it at a neighbor's where sugar making was already established, or in selling it as seed cane for new plantations of that kind. It is mainly in those two districts that for many years indigo was least productive, but sugar has now brought back prosperity to those areas where barren lands foretold only the owner's destitution and his creditor's despair.

I shall not repeat what I have said about sugar in my observations on agriculture; my opinion is unchanged in that regard. But there remains a very interesting experiment to be made in Lower Louisiana, that is to try the sugarcane of Otahiti which produces there an excellent grade, and matures at least a month earlier. And if some is imported and then increased by several years of planting, there will soon be enough to attempt the satisfactory production of this sugarcane.

When I speak of numerous slaveholdings in Louisiana, I do not mean to say that individual planters here have as many slaves as on sugar plantations in the tropical colonies. The smallest plantations in the tropics had as many slaves as the largest in Louisiana, where there are perhaps only two sugar plantations with eighty slaves. The average ones have from forty to fifty, and there are some that manufacture sugar with less than twelve slaves, and even provide facilities for neighbors that are not as prosperous. The obstacles to the importation of Negroes into the province have been quite harmful to that kind of establishment. Even so, many inhabitants do not at all regret having taken on a crop that requires such a large number of workers. On the other hand, they do not expect much results from cotton whose success seems to be affected, if not by the elevation of the land, at least by the large extent of swamplands surrounding them that increase the swarms of insects or adversely affect the weather. In any case, the proximity of Tchoupitoulas and the First German Parish to New Orleans and its growing port will in due time and by preference assure them a source of supplies which they can profitably exchange for their lumber, rice, corn, and other products.

From the Second German Parish and upward there are fewer sugar plantations. Untilled lands would still provide some means for the cultivation of indigo, and attempts at growing cotton have sufficiently come up to the planter's expectations. There are at least as many whites in that district, I believe, as there are blacks. There are quite a large number of those old German families who in former years gave their name to that portion of the banks along the Mississippi. Also settled in that parish are more of those Acadians who came from Nantes and the United States after the peace of 1783, and they too were spread further up the river among the different parishes that remain for me to describe.

After this comes the parish of Cantrelle, better known by that name although there are some who use the one with which the church has baptized it.[26] This parish has fewer sugar plantations than the preceding one, and there are none further up; but on the other hand, cotton has snatched from misery and despair a large part of those Acadian families that had been relegated there, and who hardly have any slaves. Several wealthy persons in that connection exercise a kind of vassalage over them by the means they have of buying their early fruits and vegetables but soon the Acadians will enjoy all the advantages of increased wealth and will enrich themselves by a cultivation, even more advantageous, that does not require the setting up of slave quarters nor owning slaves.

Moreover, children and old people can gather these products without getting very tired, thus enabling the father of a family to see his fortune increase in proportion to the number of his children.

Beyond the parish of Cantrelle is Lafourche Parish, similar in products and population, although the latter parish enjoys quite an advantage in its rate of growth.[27] It is in the center of Lafourche Parish on the right bank of the Mississippi that the bayou of the same name has its source, and it is on the rather high banks of this bayou that some new plantations, resettled from other locations, were established several years ago, whose crops more than meet the planter's expectation, and bring the government's attention to the wealth which could be realized by colonists along so many other bayous whose availablility has not been made known. Bayou Lafourche is already bordered by cultivated lands for quite a distance from its source at the Mississippi. Its branches on the left bank connect with the bayous and lakes of Barataria, and those of the right bank lead to the Attakapas post by joining with the waters of Bayou Plaquemines, while its overflow pours into the Gulf between *L'Anse aux Bois* and Ascension Bay.[28] The settlements on its banks will extend someday as far as the Gulf, and as long as there will be the need to portage at the bayou's source at the Mississippi during low water— which disadvantage the government has thus far done nothing to alleviate—it is the bayou's outlet into the Gulf that will one day assure their prosperity. And then its products destined for the New Orleans market will frequently be seen entering the mouth of the river.

The parish of Manchac is the next above Lafourche Parish; less extensive and not as populated as the latter, it also owes the prosperity, that has just replaced poverty in its homes throughout the parish, to the cultivation of cotton. Its principal community is near the source of Iberville Bayou or River at the Mississippi, which connects with the lakes during flood stage of the Mississippi, completing the circle of water around New Orleans which is why some early voyagers were told that it was built on an island.[29] It is at this post that the English had established headquarters, or rather an anchorage, for the commerce which they carried on with Louisiana from the time of its possession by the Spaniards until the capture of this post and Pensacola toward the end of the penultimate war.[30] Their merchant ships were usually supposed to go up the river as far as the Iberville River, but they hardly had passed New Orleans by more than three miles when they anchored, even tied up to the shore, and were able to trade their cargoes. It was, as I have previously observed when speaking of agriculture, a favorable time for the Louisiana planter which, however, ended when the English withdrew; it is to be hoped that his success will establish itself on more solid foundations.[31]

Nine leagues above Bayou Lafourche, on the right bank, the parish of Manchac has an opening from the Mississippi into Bayou Plaquemines, which could also give it a means of expansion, but the navigation is obstructed by logs which the river carries there and which creates a quite considerable logjam. The branches of that bayou extend to the Attakapas and Opelousas posts and flow upward to join the Atchafalaya River, which then passes through those two fertile districts of Lower Louisiana. More than anything else, Bayou Plaquemines and its branches provide Manchac Parish with communication to Lower Louisiana, and if the care and supervision of the government is successful in breaking up the logjams formed by the river, it would drain vast extents of land that border Bayou Plaquemines and its branches and bring life to their banks. The destruction of the logjams blocking the flow of the bayou interests all the Attakapas and Opelousas property owners, whose districts have already spent enormous sums to facilitate its navigation. But left to their own resources, without actual encouragement on the part of the government, their efforts have not produced any decided improvements. The necessity to portage goods, coupled with the inaccessibility of Bayou Plaquemines to the Mississippi at low stage, works against the growth of these districts as much in wealth as in population. And rising waters caused by clogged streams not only create more mud flats in the rear areas of settlements along the river, but perhaps also contribute to the frequent overflowing of its banks. Bayou Plaquemines flows into the Gulf in a more circuitous direction than Bayou Lafourche after having, in its course or by its branches, combined with or joined the same bayou and numerous little lakes. These form with Bayou Plaquemines the borders of, or penetrate into, the Attakapas country, and, by their flow, enlarge various streams which I shall describe. Finally, the discouragement of the planter and indifference of the government result in the abandonment of that valuable communication which, soon unusable in all its course, will fill to overflowing the planter's despair because he is compelled to take another route, and, at the same time, will expose the government's mistakes in its denial of improvements of which the bayou is capable.

Just above the parish of Manchac is Baton Rouge Parish, less populated by Acadians, richer in slaves, but similar in products. Among its inhabitants there are several English families still wealthy from the commerce that they carried on with the colony; and on the left bank on the higher ground where the ridge begins, there are several scattered sparse settlements of former subjects from the United States. They could expand considerably on both banks, for if the left bank has no mud flats as in other parts of Lower Louisiana, the right bank, despite that disadvantage, is also susceptible to a very large development in its crops and population. In these various matters, generally speaking, the parish can hardly compare with those which adjoin the city, but it possesses the resources eventually to rival them.

In case of hostilities with the United States, troops could be assembled on the highlands of the left bank starting at Baton Rouge, and could reach there in boats or overland. It is there also that the Spanish government has thought it advisable to build a fort after having established the boundaries with the United States decreed in their last treaty. The security of the province even more urgently required this fort because its neighbors were assembling at the same time the army that I mentioned in my preceding observations on government. I shall not dwell upon the unpardonable mistakes in the overall effect and situation of that insignificant fort. Located on the upper part of the bend in the river, it seems to have been destined exclusively to repulse forces going up the river rather than attacks of an enemy descending it. This fort, which in fact could not garrison half a battalion, required a greater size, and more imagination in its arrangement; for if it should defend the road on the right bank, and sink all the enemy ships that would attempt to go down the river, it should also protect the access to the highland on the left bank below Baton Rouge that is the only route to New Orleans. It would accordingly allow time, by its resistance in case it ran the risk of being captured, for troops to come station themselves on both banks at the many narrow places where an army would find itself continually cut to pieces by a few artillery companies, and which it would not be able to avoid without throwing itself on one side into the hazardous marshes, or drowning on the other side in the waters of the Mississippi.

In order to be fortified, all the settlements on the river above Baton Rouge would require enormous expenditures, and I should dare say, unnecessary, since they are for the most part isolated and could not afford garrisons (ruinous in their cost of upkeep) large enough to resist an army of several thousand men. Their inhabitants, if they are encouraged, would one day provide the means to resist attack, but assuming an approaching invasion by the United States, what would it matter if they might seize for the time being those various settlements? They could even seize, if it was their wish, settlements on the north shore of Lake Maurepas and Lake Pontchartrain; they would wander about in the pine forests, and they would still find insurmountable obstacles if they wanted to penetrate toward Mobile and Pensacola. If the state of Kentucky, the part of Pennsylvania bordering on the Ohio, the settlements on the right bank of the Tennessee River, the Tennessee and Cumberland districts, and finally Natchez, so close to New Orleans—all became a party to an undertaking, as impolitic as it would be disastrous and ruinous for their agriculture and commerce, what would be their future? New Orleans, supreme mistress and unassailable at the mouth of the Mississippi, could make them submit to terms for the export of their products. Furthermore, if the other American states suffered reverses at the hands of Spain, there would remain for the areas mentioned above, to atone for their error [in attacking Louisiana] only the option of either being recognized as Spanish subjects before their basic interests would have dictated, or to reimburse the Spanish government for all the expenses of their unsuccessful war.

East of Baton Rouge, on the left bank of the Amite River, into which Bayou Iberville or Manchac flows, near its mouth at Lake Maurepas, there is a settlement known as Galveston. Its name comes from Governor [Don Bernardo de] Gálvez, under whose command Lower Louisiana conquered these lands and Pensacola [1779–1781] from the English. Although the surrounding country reflects the fertility of the river banks, especially in ascending the Amite River, its settlements have not flourished in proportion to those which I have mentioned. Bayou Cornet, which flows through the best land of that section, is also quite populated along its banks; and, on the streams or bayous in the direction of the lakes on the north shore, there are scattered settlements that stand out among the lofty pine forests and have fertile pastures around them.

Immediately above Baton Rouge, on the left bank, is New Feliciana, a district bounded on the north by the border between Louisiana and the United States. That area consists of settlements on Bayous Feliciana or White Bluff, Alexander, Sara, Tunica, and others. Seven-eights of the population, some of whom came from Natchez, are former British or United States subjects, while the others are generally of those Canadian families [Acadians] of whom I have already spoken. The chances for prosperity for that parish are as good as in the others. Cotton has become the basic crop, and for the last three years an increase in the population of both races has assured the importance of this section of Lower Louisiana, and in that connection has placed it on the same level as the above mentioned parishes, hardly varying in number by more than 2,000 to 3,000 individuals of all colors. In general, there are in this district highlands with excellent soil prevailing for some distance back from the bayous, and which reach back to the pine forests that cover a large part of the Floridas, and can also provide some pitch and tar. All the bayous are navigable during the season of high water, and Bayou Sara is navigable all the year, even as far as twelve to fifteen leagues during low water in small boats. The air is healthful, the sites are agreeable, and one enjoys an advantage unknown in the swampy part of Lower Louisiana: that of finding delicious spring water. In the New Feliciana district there remain to be settled a considerable amount of lands superior to those on the north side of the lakes, of which they are an extension as described in my references to the Floridas and adjacent territories.[32]

I come now to the last settlement of Lower Louisiana along the banks of the Mississippi: Pointe Coupée, on the right bank facing the preceding district, named thus because it is a point of land that was cut off from the left bank when the river changed its course many years ago. The district of the old bank is still as important as the one that now borders the river. They are separated by a swamp that nobody has attempted to fill up or drain, and the old river bed along the settlements of False River contains drainage water and seepage that connects it through the back country with the branches of Bayou Plaquemines. This rich parish, like those which adjoin the city, has a rather large disproportion of whites and blacks, numbering about 2,000 blacks against 700 to 800 whites, and 60 to 80 free people of color. Before the cultivation of cotton, indigo still sustained the prosperity of that settlement, but soon it had shared the anxiety and misery of others, and several wealthy individuals there found themselves surrounded by unfortunates from whom they were able to buy up at a ridiculous price the lands and miserable slaveholdings. Fortunately, cotton has received from the soil and commerce the favors withheld from indigo, and there, more than in any other section of the colony, plantation owners have made, by the high price of the new commodity they cultivated, up to 30 percent on their capital. That settlement, like those previously mentioned, is capable of important improvements and developments.

Bounded on the west by the Atchafalaya River that extends also to the Mississippi at the thirty-first parallel, Pointe Coupée would be the first to enjoy the effects of the drainage that could be undertaken, and its communication with the interior would be easy and fast. Through thrift, good order, field hands, and encouragements, the government will then not only assure itself the possession of Lower Louisiana, but also its prosperity.

I end my description of this area on the Atchafalaya River in order to proceed to the Attakapas and Opelousas districts in the southwest, but I shall return to describe it in great detail. The view that the map [Map of a Portion of Lower

Louisiana and West Florida] gives of the rivers, lakes, and bayous in those two districts cannot be considered as perfect. It presents an idea of the many means of access that actually exist and that in Attakapas particularly offer the greatest advantage for developing the settlements. I had indeed many exact reports in that regard, but for reasons that I have already explained, I have not been able to secure for myself a plan quite correct in its details.

The vast district of Attakapas, located about forty leagues from New Orleans traveling by way of Bayou Lafourche and following its branches toward the southwest, is separated from the Gulf, as far as the vicinity of the mouth of Bayou Teche, by a narrow extension of the marshy prairies of Barataria that will develop one day from their periodic fills and drainage. Commencing at the Gulf, arable lands of this district extend to the northeast on the left bank of the Teche, and veer toward the north for about thirty leagues. The lands of Opelousas form its western boundary beyond the Mermentau River. All the streams in this district, including the Vermillion River which is between the Mermentau and the Teche, feel the effects of the tides, and they are all more or less navigable. The Mermentau, which does not yet have any settlements along it, presents, so they believe, more possibilities for navigation than the other two rivers. They are, however, not without some important resources in that respect, since they are building on their banks at this moment (March, 1802) three schooners of ninety tons burden, and they have repaired one that has already made some voyages to New Orleans in passing through the Gulf to the mouth of the Mississippi. Except for the war, that water route would have taken on an even greater activity for the commerce and inhabitants of this district; and the precious time that was lost—by the difficult task of going up the bayous leading to New Orleans in transporting such bulk cargoes as sugar, cotton, tobacco, and salt provisions—will be used in establishing and maintaining their plantations.

Quite a few islands emerge from the sandbar that parallels, only a short distance out, all the shores of the Gulf of Mexico. Many of these islands are not even shown on any map. One of them, facing the bay of the Teche River whose pass into the Gulf is better than that of Vermillion River, is called *Belle Isle*, whose high ground, thickly wooded and quite fertile, provides a twofold advantage in forming a bay: a safe harbor under its shelter and the natural protection of the port that this fertile country will one day require. A sailor who has often been there assures me that some usable channels at *Pointe au Fer* are never less than eight feet deep at low tide, and he confirms that there are some deeper ones, expecially at a place called *Pointe au Chevreuil*.

Several inhabitants have been successful in establishing themselves on *Belle Isle*, but on the mainland they are starting settlements only at a place several miles from the mouths of the Teche and Vermillion rivers, the lands bordering the Teche being of better quality than those along the Vermillion. According to the generally unanimous reports on that area, there is no doubt that it is a country which unites all the attractiveness of location and climate to the fertility of the soil. Behind the streams' high banks, covered with very fine forests, there are some superb plains sheltered from all floods. The traveler has a delightful view of a large expanse that varies from the Gulf side with its beach and offshore islands, to the land side with its occasional wooded slopes, or the banks of small streams on which clusters of trees seem to rise up expressly to beautify the countryside. The spring waters there are good; fishing is quite plentiful because of the proximity to the Gulf, and hunting, in its variety and ease, makes it a sportsman's delight.

Cotton is grown successfully in the Attakapas country, and the establishment of several sugar plantations has proven that sugarcane, favored by a climate where the winter is still infinitely less damaging than on the banks of the Mississippi, promises more dependable results there. None of the lands in those parts have ever been planted in indigo. They raise a large quantity of domestic animals of all kinds that provide nine-tenths of the needs of agriculture and the supplies for butchers in Lower Louisiana. It is possible to cultivate advantageously all the products that other sections of the province supply to New Orleans markets, even corn, flax, and hemp. The incentives of peace will bring plentiful amounts of salt beef and pork, and to be of good quality they only require that the producers receive instructions which those with experience have not been able to give them. I could go on indefinitely if I repeated all that has been told me, without exception, by those who have visited that district where the difficulties of transportation isolate the population and where on 800 to 900 square leagues of surface there are perhaps not more than 3,000 whites and 1,500 blacks.

It is in the Attakapas district that the Spanish government formerly had a slight inclination to do something about its development. It wanted to establish a town under the name of New Iberia in the center of such a fine country, but the measures taken to that end were so effective and so sustained that there remains only the memory of the attempt which was made! The parish of the district is now located seven leagues further up, and about ten leagues from the border of the Opelousas district. I do not know in what circumstances Spain originally conceived this project, but I repeat again that it was abandoned after a reversal of her politics with regard to Louisiana. Spain would have persisted if she had been able to populate the district exclusively with real Spaniards—as it was, people of French origin settled there and grew in numbers—and already perhaps there would no longer be any wilderness between that district, the province of Texas, and Nacogdoches.

The Opelousas district, bordering the Attakapas district on the west and northwest surpasses it in area, is as good as it is

in richness of soil and climate advantages; but is less populated because it is further away from New Orleans. Bayou
Plaquemines, in its neglected condition with logjams as mentioned above, is their sole means of communication by boat.
The combined population of the Attakapas and Opelousas
districts consists of 5,000 whites and 2,000 slaves. Thus, a
more extensive district could be formed there that would
have the following borders: in the east, the Attakapas district
and the lands which the logjams of the Atchafalaya keep
flooding; in the north, the lands of the Avoyelles post on the
Red River; in the northwest, those of Natchitoches on the
same river; in the west, the Sabine River which separates, they
say, the provinces of Texas and Louisiana; and, to the south,
the shores of the Gulf for a distance of thirty to forty leagues.

The Opelousas district that is along the Gulf presents the
same appearance as most of the Attakapas: fertile and well-
irrigated lands, charming scenery, immense prairies; everything, in fact, inviting the planter there to a life of complete
enjoyment. If this district is cut off by its location from
communication with the chain of lakes and bayous that
provide an outlet for the products of the inhabited section in
the Attakapas country, nature by way of compensation has
irrigated it with several streams which, similar to those of the
Teche and the Vermillion, would carry its commodities down
to the Gulf and receive products in exchange by the same
route. Besides the Mermentau River, of which I have spoken,
it has the Calcasieu River situated almost at the center of its
shores, and according to the reports of a Mr. I. Elliott, who
discovered it more than fifteen years ago, it can have at its
mouth one of the most advantageous ports of those regions.[33]
The Opelousas district with all these advantages only needs
slaves for it to prosper and if, as there is no reason to doubt at
least during times of peace, the attempts at navigation on the
Teche are successful they will soon be transported there by
that means.

The remaining surface of the Opelousas district is higher

than the shores that I have just described, but it is not as varied or picturesque as the major portion of the Attakapas district. Some pleasant slopes have their contours watered by the numerous springs that form the headwaters of the streams flowing through these two districts. Each plantation, so to speak, can have one of these small streams serve as its boundary and as an outlet for its commodities during high water. But lacking access to the Gulf, the population has necessarily established itself only on the eastern portion of the Opelousas district where, either by portage or transferring from one waterway to another, they can pass from the upper reaches of the Teche and Vermillion rivers to the Atchafalaya, Bayous Fordocher [Fordoche], Courtableau, and Plaquemines, and finally to the Mississippi.

The products of the Attakapas and Opelousas districts should be similar, as indeed they really are; and several million individuals should one day be happy there with the richness of the soil and the climate's mildness. And to convince one's self of the area's excellence it is enough to say that whether the penniless individual or the securely rich man living a peaceful rural life goes there, neither one longs to come back to the mud holes of New Orleans, despite the attraction its luxury and dissipation can provide, and notwithstanding the precarious, tiring, and expensive means of communications.

Attakapas and Opelousas are the names of former Indian tribes who occupied these fine countries. One still sees some survivors who, peaceful and somewhat civilized, keep themselves busy either by farming or navigation on the waterways. Similar survivors of the Chetimachas, Tonikas, Alabamans, and other Indian tribes are also found in those districts and on the banks of the Atchafalaya and the branches of Bayou Plaquemines. To the west of the two districts, beyond the Sabine River, along the Trinity River and in other regions, are still found various Indian tribes, whose names I shall not mention, as useless as they are barbarous, who live in peace with the Spaniards, and whose savagery was displayed so many times against the ships that misfortune had caused to enter St. Bernard Bay.

I come back now to the Atchafalaya River whose details, I have said above, concern the physical and political existence of Lower Louisiana. If it is undeniable that the lands of Lower Louisiana—bordered on the north, the east, and the south by the ridge that starts at Baton Rouge, the various lakes, and the Gulf; and to the west by the highlands of the Attakapas and Opelousas districts—are centuries-old alluvial deposits of the Mississippi, there is no doubt then that the large bayous were its mouths at one time or another. And the Atchafalaya which always receives some water from the Mississippi during the low as well as the high stage, can be considered at present as a branch of that river by the distance it has to flow to empty into the Gulf. Starting at the thirty-first parallel just beyond the mouth of the Red River, with a width that I believe is more than 100 *toises* [213 yards], and of a great depth, it follows a course directly south, makes a large bend twenty-five or thirty leagues further downstream, flows to the right and left into the various bayous that I have already described, forms islands and little lakes, empties in large part into the Teche and finally carries the rest of its waters into the Gulf a short distance from the mouth of that river. In any event, those are my conclusions from all the information I have gathered regarding areas for which no accurate maps yet exist.

For the last twenty-five years an accumulation of branches and tree trunks, brought by the swift current to a place in the Atchafalaya twenty leagues from its source, has held fast and consolidated to such an extent, while increasing every year, that it threatens to close this river from there back to the banks of the Mississippi. In addition, as the Atchafalaya still provides an important outlet, the logjam may cause the excess water that it was able to take to flow back into the

Mississippi. Nevertheless, this mass of water must find an outlet. During low water it seeps through the accumulated wood, and at high water in winter and spring inundates the natural springs, fills up the bayous and swamps, and tends to raise the level of streams whose low water was probably caused mainly by the logjams. The district that the Atchafalaya flows through further down has nothing to fear from those handicaps. They do, however, already result in some real difficulties on the banks of the Mississippi, and threaten even more serious ones if steps are not taken to clear out the fifteen leagues of accumulated wood that obstructs the Atchafalaya, or if the Mississippi in a violent surge opens up a new outlet that could perhaps also cause some extensive devastations.

The destruction of fifteen leagues of clogged wood seems today, if not an impossibility at least a very large undertaking. The inhabitants of the Opelousas and Attakapas districts are not fearful that their settlements can be flooded by the Atchafalaya, but only in the Opelousas district are they concerned about the logjams reforming further downstream where the reopening and branching out of its course takes place. This newly formed logjam might close to them the mouths of bayous Fordocher, Courtableau, and Plaquemines that are actually their only means of communication with New Orleans. That event would have grave consequences if they really could not avoid isolating out of existence a district that should someday become of great importance. But if necessity requires that attention be given to the banks of the Mississippi threatened with flooding by its rising waters near the Atachafalaya's source, and if political considerations do not any less urgently require a European government [Spain] to settle a large population in the Opelousas district, and to improve its soil to help them achieve success, then there is no doubt that it would also concern itself with the means of avoiding new accumulations of clogged wood on the Atchafalaya, and at the same time assure communications with the two districts that would facilitate access to the Gulf. Thus, there is no reason why navigation of the Atchafalaya should not be kept open.

If the Atchafalaya started to accumulate wood debris in its course twenty to twenty-five years ago while different bayous became stopped up or clogged, since about that same time the waters of the Mississippi have risen to a height unknown until then. The various reports seem to confirm the accuracy of that statement, and leave no doubt upon reflection that the cause of this phenomenon—which seems contrary to the way nature normally acts in countries where the population and farming increase progressively—results from cutting off, beyond relative proportions, the Mississippi's branches and outlets which were available during high water.

The years 1800 and 1801, whose river crests did not reach the height now considered normal, should not be taken as an exception to the above remarks. A few idle storytellers or some dreamers have gratuitously attributed the low-water stage during those last two years to I don't know what convulsion of nature, occasioned by the terrible eruption of a volcano near the headwaters of the great Missouri River, which, changing the course of various rivers near the Pacific Ocean, diminished the volume of water that it furnishes annually to the Mississippi. But the year 1802 has just completely destroyed that fable. The waters of the Mississippi from the Atchafalaya to its mouth have risen more than ever before, and in twenty places have carried away the dikes or levees (that latter term being more commonly used in the colony). As I finish these *Observations* [May, 1802] the overflow has been stopped in many other places by quickly building a small embankment on top of the levee. But the anxious colonist still doubted that the Missouri emptied into the Mississippi, and in that case would no longer contribute to making his ruin inevitable. It was altogether natural to suppose that during 1800 and 1801—which should not nullify the experience of the previous twenty consecutive years—the rain, ice, and snow which regularly swell the waters of the Mississippi and its tributaries in springtime, had given less moisture only because of a very unusual exception during the course of the season, by causes that belong to the study of the winds. For could it not be reasonably assumed that the moisture produced by the constant evaporation on the varying surfaces of the Great Lakes that together form more than 20,000 square leagues, that the moisture, I say, which should furnish so much water to the rivers of that portion of America had been flowing toward the Atlantic or Pacific oceans in such a way as to diminish the sources of the volume of water flowing into the Mississippi? Does not nature provide many examples to justify that exception in 1800 and 1801, which the Mississippi had never before experienced in its usual condition of flood waters in Lower Louisiana?

Deprived of a portion of the two largest outlets that remain to it for its high water by the logjams of the Atchafalaya and Bayou Plaquemines, the Mississippi owes the increase in its rising waters to another reason: the levees that are intended to keep it within its two banks have, in their progressive extensions, worked with the disadvantages mentioned above to so confine it that devastating floods are bound to come. In the face of all this, there is no doubt that the government should do something immediately.

Shortly after the founding of New Orleans, when agriculture started to establish itself along the banks of the river, the lands that seemed to be less exposed to flooding were the only ones that attracted the attention of new colonists. As their numbers increased and the assistance they could secure from being near the capital caused them to stay close by, they became less particular about their choice; they thought with reason that other lands more exposed could, nevertheless, also be put into cultivation provided some precautions were taken. They realized that in building a levee, three, four, or five feet high, even more, on the banks of the river, depending upon local conditions, they could profitably use nearly all the land along both banks—except in those places where a deep ravine would have required too high a levee to be built by their own laborers or combined with those of other planters. Originally the building of levees was only at intervals subject to the landowner's whim, but the favorable results, having demonstrated their usefulness, made them a general requirement; then levees became a primary condition in consideration for which one could obtain land concessions.

The levees were extended more and more without interruption for some distance from the capital; and, at intervals, as far as the cutoff at Pointe Coupée, some isolated sections were built just after the peace of 1783. In approaching New Orleans the river formed, in places where there were interruptions to its flow, especially in the lowlands, some bays into which part of its high water flowed. As a result of this diversion, the settlements were not inundated. About that time the Acadian families arrived; they were widely dispersed among the different parishes, extending as far up as the Atchafalaya, and where most of them were condemned for many years to fruitless labors because of the need to contend with, maintain, or reconstruct levees along the Mississippi. That river, being more contained and not able to overflow its banks, poured with more force into the bayous where they had not been able to dam its outlet, carying along an even larger quantity of driftwood and logs, and creating obstructions which, by increasing the pressure of the water in the narrow stream that the levees gave to the Mississippi's course, often caused some very extensive floods.

The overflow which results from the narrowing of the Mississippi and the logjams on the Atchafalaya and Bayou Plaquemines occurs much further away than Lower Louisiana. The Red River and the Ouachita, which have a common outlet at the Mississippi immediately above the Atchafalaya, are the first to feel the effects, and their floods have greatly increased in depth since these various channels are clogged. There was formerly, rather close to the mouth of the Red River, a fort that the French had built before the cession of the province, which no longer exists and which by reason of the increase in high water could no longer survive. Some vast prairies along the Ouachita, named prairies of Vilmont, Lee, and so on, others on the Red River, lands extending just about sixty leagues between these rivers, are more or less flooded by that overflow. The prairies which I have just mentioned had the beginnings of some settlements before that handicap, and they would now be habitable only by building levees similar to those of Lower Louisiana.

As long as most of the inhabitants of Louisiana languished along the banks of the Mississippi, it was not found necessary to worry about high water. The lack of means among some, the despair of others, caused them to abandon or neglect the building up or maintenance of levees. And Spain, whose simple possession of Louisiana satisfied her needs, deliberately saw the devastation by flooding without deeming it necessary to concern herself with seeking its cause. But now that the colonist is no longer under the threat of worthlessness or failure of indigo; that sugar and cotton, even in times of war, restore his courage and his fortune; that he is more interested in the proper upkeep of the levees; that politics direct the Europeans to make Louisiana flourish in order to retain it—at this time, I say, will not Spain be alarmed by the destruction which a much greater overflow of water could cause when Bayou Plaquemines and the Atchafalaya become completely clogged, and when even Bayou Lafourche will necessarily be narrowed because of farming along its banks? Will Spain not realize the need to facilitate drainage and communications? Will she not, finally, occupy herself with the means to secure for Lower Louisiana—which owes the glimmer of prosperity that it enjoys to the courage of its inhabitants—the advantages, population, wealth, and security which should cause its government to be respected, and place limits on the ambition of its neighbors?

I believe that the details which I have just gone into will sufficiently prove my assertion regarding the importance of the Atchafalaya, and the need to destroy its logjams and those of Bayou Plaquemines. A foot of water lower at New Orleans, even six inches, resulting from opening those two streams, would increase the water level in the Atchafalaya by several feet and, no longer leaving the planters along the Mississippi's banks in anxiety, would drain a considerable stretch of swamps throughout the province. They talk about the impossibility of achieving that, and they believe on oath several hunters who alone have seen the logjams, and perhaps have exaggerated their height and length. But let them send some experts and European engineers there with competent laborers and equipment, and soon, either by using crowbars or torches they will restore a branch of the Mississippi in the Atchafalaya, provide a more considerable outflowing through Bayou Plaquemines, and find a reliable way to avoid new logjams. Then they could concern themselves with drainage, increase the cultivated lands, and effectively work toward improvement of navigation on the Mississippi and in keeping open its passes into the Gulf. Perhaps then another port will finally be established at the mouth of the Teche, which the rich lands of the Opelousas and Attakapas districts will help prosper, and which could receive, through several tributaries of the Atchafalaya, its share of the large amount of products which the upper reaches of the Mississippi give promise of sending down.

After having dwelt at length on a point that I consider as very important, particularly for Lower Louisiana, I am going to resume my topographical description starting at the thirty-first parallel where I had interrupted myself. Since all of the settlements on the left bank of the Mississippi are now subject to the government of the United States, I shall first speak of all those on the right bank that belong to Spain and sustain themselves under her government in destitution, mediocrity, and with a stagnant population.

Just beyond the Atchafalaya is the Red River, flowing from the northwest. Its waters, brackish in taste for a reason which I shall have occasion to explain, join with the Ouachita on the left bank ten leagues from where they flow into the Mississippi. For a distance of twenty leagues northwest to the post of Avoyelles on the right bank, the Red River floods both banks and, as mentioned earlier, this results from its own rising waters as well as from the Mississippi's overflow. With the poor quality of its water, which one can hardly drink when the Red River is low, is coupled the difficulty of its navigation. But the beautiful banks of the Red River and their rich soil, together with the important communications which it can establish, will benefit the prosperity of the province at all times. From Avoyelles to Rapides, another post on the Red River, which takes its name from the shoals that obstruct its navigation during low water and often interfere with it even during high water, the distance is somewhat more than twenty leagues; and though both are capable of development, they are still much less important than Natchitoches located forty leagues farther up. The combined population of the three settlements mentioned above amounts to about 2,500 whites and 1,200 blacks; and the principal product consisted for a long time of tobacco, which was in great demand because of its good reputation. The government bought it from them under contract, and using as an excuse the fraud in overcharging on the part of a few inhabitants made them all disappointed with the income from their tobacco, or suddenly discontinuing taking any at all, put them in the position of having to sell to others at low price, and even brought them to the threshold of poverty. Fortunately, the successful growing of cotton on their land has brought benefits. The large amount of plug tobacco, not moving to market because of the government's refusal to buy it, was exported, and their future assorted harvests of tobacco, cotton, and some pelts, will provide encouraging results.

The increase in population and prosperity which the banks of the Red River could attain is incalculable, for it extends for more than 300 leagues from the Mississippi to its source in the mountains that the Louisianians call the Cados Mountains just beyond Santa Fe, capital of the kingdom of New Mexico.[34] From Avoyelles to the Grand Cados (about 150 leagues) the banks of the river, varying in extent, consist generally of excellent land where nature has favorably mingled vast plains covered with cane or native rush, majestic forests, and common prairies. Along these same Cados, on the right and left of the river, is the beginning of immense plains that, on the northern side, extend to the banks of the Arkansas River in passing by the headwaters of the Ouachita, and on the southern side, they extend as far as the frontiers of the province of Texas—plains on which are found thousands of cattle and wild horses, the first mentioned especially near the province of Texas.

On an island in the middle of the Red River, 120 to 130 leagues beyond the Cados, there is a rock of salt that supplies many of the Indian tribes, those located nearby selling it to the others. Presumably, it is mainly there that the Red River acquires the brackish quality in its water, receiving also in its course, as far as the Mississippi, the drainage of the lakes and salt springs which are located between it and the Ouachita. Continually wide and fordable everywhere, it finally reaches to the Cados Mountains that I have mentioned, in the vicinity of which, toward the east and north, four or five other large streams flowing into the Mississippi or the Missouri, also have their source.

By one of those impediments which betrays Spain's policy with respect to Louisiana, communication with New Mexico, that nature provides by the Red River, is forbidden. Not only is the entry of merchandise prohibited by that route, but the frontier itself can be crossed by a traveler only with a passport, very difficult to obtain. And permission to go there in order to trade for the innumerable wild horses that roam the plains, in the first place can be secured only at the whim of the viceroy of Mexico, a great and rare favor on his part, and then with a bribe to the government of Louisiana. The easiest way that one can embark on this kind of speculation is to take advantage of an occasion to visit Vera Cruz to risk the selling of some contraband merchandise for gold, and purchase (for there is a price for everything) a passport to return by way of the interior provinces. At the frontier gold can be exchanged for mules and horses which actually cost very little, but they must be led 400 to 500 leagues through forests where there is always the threat of being robbed either by the sellers or Indians.

If the colony changes government, the situation of the Natchitoches post will also improve considerably in importance through the contraband trade carried on with New Mexico. The route to the border is easy, and the one to Santa Fe, now well known, can be covered in thirty-five days at most, even with pack horses. A frontier post of that realm (Nacogdoches) is at the center of a country similar to the Opelousas district, and is only fifty leagues southwest of Natchitoches. San Antonio, in the same line, capital of the province of Texas, is not even 200 leagues distant, and the route to it passes through fertile lands irrigated by the Trinity and other rivers. And in the attempts at trade which could be initiated, smugglers would have been pleased with the profitable results if only they had been able to depend, during the round trip, on protection provided by Louisiana authorities. But as Louisiana is also under Spanish control, the smuggler found that its officials were enemies spying on him, and his judges. The banks of the Rio Bravo and those of its branches are rapidly becoming settled. Gold is already plentiful there, and on a frontier of 200 to 300 leagues, impossible to guard, there are meeting places for the exchange of goods to which the Mexican will travel even more readily since the commerce of Louisiana, in realizing a considerable profit, will supply him with first-class merchandise at a price 100 percent cheaper than can be had at Vera Cruz and other distant Mexican ports where cargoes arrive from Spanish ports after having been handled three or four times.

The Natchitoches district could also be the location for an establishment that would give support to its commerce, but which for political reasons Spain has not encouraged, that is, a monopoly trading privilege with the Indians whose way of life causes them to stay along the rivers of the area, and for most of whom the name of "Frenchman" is still held in esteem. Such, for instance, as those west of the Natchitoches district who inhabit the forests of the province of Texas and send several representatives annually to visit the commandant to recall the memory of the first French captain who subjected them, and whom they still call their "First Father and Benefactor" [Juchereau de St. Denis].

The Indians near the settlements of the Natchitoches district are some scattered survivors of those that formerly inhabited Lower Louisiana or West Florida, and who spend more time at work than in hunting. But in ascending the Red River beyond the Cados Mountains, it is evident that the Osage War and smallpox have reduced the number of other Indian tribes near whose location the trading company could establish a branch with the added advantage of also being close to the Santa Fe Trail. It would attract there the wandering tribes that follow the herds on the magnificent prairies which start beyond the Cados, and it could trade with those proud Ayetanes [Apaches], sworn enemies of the Spaniards and always at war with them, who roam in large bands in the Cados Mountains and on the frontiers of New Mexico. In approaching the plains one sees, from the river's highlands and its borders, only immense herds of buffalo, deer, stags, and other animals. Bears are quite common in the wooded areas; there are more crocodiles beyond the Cados; many beavers and otters on the shores of the streams, lakes, and swamps; and the wild game is just as plentiful. One finally arrives at the Cados Mountains where the Indian arms himself in his war garb in order to hunt the grizzly bear, more dangerous than the other species, found there in abundance and whose claws are used by the Indians to make necklaces or other ornaments for ostentatious display.

One advantage that the company trading with the Indians could also offer in that area for the profit of the province would be to attract—by a route that is shorter, easier, and safer—an abundance of pelts which the nomadic Indians, such as the Osages and the Kampes [Kansa], take to the monopoly traders along the streams which flow into the Missouri River, and whose headwaters are in the Cados Mountains. That arrangement would very likely curtail some of the opportunities for smuggling which the present situation provides in the Illinois district. Moreover, in order to augment fur trapping and gain for itself the allegiance of most of the Indians on the left bank of the Mississippi, a new government could readily accede to the demands that several tribes have made to cross over to the right bank, leaving behind those lands where centuries of hunting and the close proximity to civilized people, have finally destroyed most of the wild game. One could, I say, move them toward the magnificent plains of the Cados, where war and smallpox have wrought great havoc, and where the profit which would result for them as well as for commerce would be a great benefit, and would assure to the governments of the allies [France and Spain] that security which the

United States, without this step, will take away from them.

I shall not describe here all the reports, true or false, that have been given to me indicating the valuable mines which appear at different places in the mountains beyond Natchitoches. The Indians or hunters have brought back a hundred mineral samples. But since one must submit, from among the still doubtful cases, the most likely specimens or facts most easily verified, I shall describe later what they have reported positively to me, and I now continue on to outline the Ouachita district.

The Ouachita River, as I have already mentioned, flows into the Red River ten leagues from the latter's mouth. The Ouachita district extends on both banks of its river in a direction parallel to the Natchitoches and Arkansas districts, whose rivers have their sources close together and restrict the Ouachita River's access to their branches thus causing it to be of limited extent. Navigation on the Ouachita is not difficult during high water, but several shallows hamper it at low stage. For about twenty leagues where the Red River, at flood stage, overflows reddish and brackish waters into it, the Ouachita is usually given the name of Black River, but further downstream its waters are of good quality and take the name of the district which they irrigate there. On the right bank a branch opens into a lake called Catahoula, near which are several settlements that floods deprive of real growth, and where the government intends to build a fort. It is the route followed to travel from Natchitoches to Natchez on the Mississippi, entering above Lake Catahoula on the Ouachita River into Bayou Tensas, which by its branches to the east across different small lakes, connects with the Concordia post that the Spaniards established facing Natchez, after having ceded the new boundaries to the United States.

To the northwest of Lake Catahoula, between the Natchitoches and Ouachita districts, are various salt springs or lakes which the inhabitants exploit for their own use. There is also a chalk quarry, some millstones, and in the angle of the left shore of Lake Catahoula with the Ouachita River a number of those mounds made carefully and in regular shapes, indicating a burial ground for the Indians who formerly lived in those regions. Each district has some of them scattered in its domain, but since the present-day Indians have not kept up that tradition, I shall refrain from saying more about it.

Boeuf River is nine leagues above Bayou Tensas on the left bank of the Ouachita; it is navigable and overflows during high water. Similar to the Tensas, it finally connects with the Mississippi in the area near the mouth of the Arcs River. Not all of its banks are flooded, and close to where it joins the Mississippi there are pine hills covered with rocks which provide some fairly good grinding stones and where there is an extensive view all around. Boeuf River leads to magnificent forests and natural prairies, and along the branches of its right bank they have recently discovered lands whose beauty and richness have so tempted several inhabitants of Natchez that they have applied for a concession in order to transport a large number of people to that area, either to provide some new Spanish subjects in good faith, or to await the take-over which the United States hopes to achieve sooner or later.

From the mouth of Boeuf River to Fort Miro, principal town of the district located 70 navigable leagues from the Red River, there are, on the left bank of the Ouachita and for a distance of nearly 150 leagues—mostly subject to cultivation because of the highlands on the right bank—various fine prairies with scattered settlements, according to whether the elevation of the land makes their cultivation possible at the present time. Beyond these prairies, there are either forests of various types of wood, pine thickets, and cypress groves, whose extent and fine quality can in fact provide for centuries of harvesting in the production of ships masts of every size. On the left bank there is Bayou Calumet, lined by a chain of hills, which, in a space of eight leagues, has a plaster quarry whose gypsum is often of the finest quality, and where attempts at mining have been most satisfactory. Further upstream, on the right bank, are the St. Cyr hills that contain iron ore, coal, and gypsum. The gypsum is often contaminated by the iron ore found there, and an attempt at mining made with a sufficient number of laborers would determine which of these minerals could become most important for the province, if not all three of them.[35]

END OF THE OBSERVATIONS

Treaty of San Lorenzo
el Real

The official text of the Treaty of San Lorenzo el Real (27 October 1795), also known as Pinckney's Treaty, after the American negotiator Thomas Pinckney of South Carolina, had a tremendous effect on American penetration into Spanish Louisiana. Because of Spain's war with France that abrogated her special trading privileges extended to Frenchmen in 1782, the colony's need for provisions could only come from the United States. Combined with this recognition, was the fact that Spain desperately needed American friendship and neutrality because of the European war in which she found herself. James Pitot refers to its importance frequently.

The text of this treaty has been reproduced in both the official English and Spanish text. The copy here is taken from David Hunter Miller (ed.), *Treaties and Other International Acts of the United States of America* (8 vols.; Washington: U. S. Government Printing Office, 1931–1948), II, 318–38. However, a handwritten copy, with both English and Spanish text, is among the archives at the Historic New Orleans Collection, and has only some very minor differences in wording and punctuation from the text below. The errors and carelessness in regard to grammar, punctuation, and spelling are all found in the original document.

TREATY OF SAN LORENZO EL REAL

His Catholic Majesty and the United States of America desiring to consolidate on a permanent basis the Friendship and good correspondence which happily prevails between the two Parties, have determined to establish by a convention several points, the settlement whereof will be productive of general advantage and reciprocal utility to both Nations.

With this intention His Catholic Majesty has appointed the most Excellent Lord Don Manuel de Godoy and Alvarez de Faria, Rios, Sanchez Zarzosa, Prince de la Paz Duke de la Alcudia Lord of the Soto de Roma and of the State of Albalá: Grandee of Spain of the first class: perpetual Regidor of the Citty of Santiago: Knight of the illustrious Order of the Golden Fleece, and Great Cross of the Royal and distinguished Spanish order of Charles the III. Commander of Valencia del Ventoso, Rivera, and Aceuchal in that of Santiago; Knight and Great Cross of the religious order of St. John: Counsellor of State: First Secretary of State and Despacho: Secretary to the Queen: Superintendent General of the Posts and High Ways: Protector of the Royal Academy of the Noble Arts, and of the Royal Societies of natural history, Botany, Chemistry, and Astronomy; Gentleman of the King's Chamber in employement: Captain General of his Armies: Inspector and Major of the Royal Corps of Body Guards

Deseando S. M. Catolica y los Estados Unidos de America consolidar de un modo permanente la buena correspondencia y amistad que felizmente reyna entre ambas Partes, han resuelto fixar por medio de un Convenio varios puntos de cuyo arreglo resultará un beneficio general, y una utilidad reciproca â los dos Paises.

Con esta mira ha nombrado S. M. Catolica al Excelentisimo Sor. Dn. Manuel de Godoy, y Alvarez de Faria, Rios, Sanchez Zarzosa, Principe de la Paz, Duque de la Alcudia: Señor del Soto de Roma, y del Estado de Albalá: Grande de España de primera clase: Regidor perpetuo de la Ciudad de Santiago: Caballero de la insigne Orden del Toyson de Oro: Gran Cruz de la Real y distinguida Orden Española de Carlos III. Comendador de Valencia del ventoso, Rivera, y Aceuchal en la de Santiago: Caballero Gran Cruz de la Religion de Sn. Juan: Consegero de Estado: primer Secretario de Estado y del Despacho: Secretario de la Reyna Nra. Sra. Superintendente general de Correos y Caminos: Protector de la Rl. Academia de las Nobles Artes, y de los Rles. Gabinere de Historia natural, Jardin Botanico, Laboratorio Chîmico, y Observatorio Astronomico: Gentilhombre de Camara con exercicio: Capitan General de los Reales Exercitos: Inspector, y Sargento Mayor del Rl. Cuerpo de Guardias de Corps. etc. etc. etc.

etc. etc. etc. and the President of the United States with the advice and consent of their Senate, has appointed Thomas Pinckney a Citizen of the United States, and their Envoy Extraordinary to his Catholic Majesty. And the said Plenipotentiaries have agreed upon and concluded the following Articles.

Art. I.

There shall be a firm and inviolable Peace and sincere Friendship between His Catholic Majesty his successors and subjects, and the United Estates and their Citizens without exception of persons or places.

Art. II.

To prevent all disputes on the subject of boundaries which separate the territories of the two High contracting Parties, it is hereby declared and agreed as follows: to wit: The Southern boundary of the United States which divides their territory from the Spanish Colonies of East and West Florida, shall be designated by a line beginning on the River Mississippi at the Northernmost part of the thirty first degree of latitude North of the Equator, which from thence shall be drawn due East to the middle of the River Apalachicola or Catahouche, thence along the middle thereof to its junction with the Flint, thence straight to the head of St. Mary's River, and thence down the middle there of to the Atlantic Occean. And it is agreed that if there should be any troops, Garrisons or settlements of either Party

y el Presidente de los Estados Unidos con el consentimiento y aprobacion del Senado à Dn. Tomas Pinckney Ciudadano de los mismos Estados y su Enviado Extraordinario cerca de S.M. Catholica. Y ambos Plenipotenciarios han ajustado y firmado los Articulos siguientes.

Art. I.

Habrá una Paz solida ê inviolable y una amistad sincera entre S. M. Catolica sus succesores y subditos, y los Estados Unidos y sus Ciudadanos, sin excepcion de personas ô lugares.

Art. II.

Para evitar toda disputa en punto â los limites que separan los territorios de las dos Altas Partes Contratantes, se han convenido, y declarado en el presente articulo lo siguiente: â saber. Que el Limite Meridional de los Estados Unidos que sepára su territorio de el de las Colonias Españolas de la Florida Occidental y de la Florida Oriental se demarcará por una linea que empieze en el Rio Misisipi en la parte mas septentrional del grado treinta y uno al Norte del Equador, y qe. desde alli siga en derechura al Este hasta el medio del Rio Apalachicola ô Catahouche, desde alli por la mitad de este Rio hasta su union con el Flint, de alli en derechura hasta el nacimiento del Rio Sta. Maria, y de alli baxando por el medio de este Rio hasta el Occeano Atlantico. Y se han convenido las dos Potencias en que si hubiese

147

in the territory of the other according to the above mentioned boundaries, they shall be withdrawn from the said territory within the term of six months after the ratification of this treaty or sooner if it be possible and that they shall be permitted to take with them all the goods and effects which they possess.

Art. III.

In order to carry the preceding Article into effect one Commissioner and one Surveyor shall be appointed by each of the contracting Parties who shall meet at the Natchez on the left side of the River Mississippi before the expiration of six months from the ratification of this convention, and they shall proceed to run and mark this boundary according to the stipulations of the said Article. They shall make Plats and keep journals of their proceedings which shall be considered as part of this convention, and shall have the same force as if they were inserted therein. And if on any account it should be found necessary that the said Commissioners and Surveyors should be accompanied by Guards, they shall be furnished in equal proportions by the Commanding Officer of his Majesty's troops in the two Floridas, and the Commanding Officer of the troops of the United States in their Southwestern territory, who shall act by common consent and amicably, as well with respect to this point as to the furnishing of provissions and

tropa, Guarniciones, ô Establecimientos de la una de las dos Partes en el territorio de la otra segun los limites que se acaban de mencionar, se retirarán de dicho territorio en el termino de seis meses despues de la ratificacion de este Tratado, ô antes si fuese posible, y que se les permitirá llevar consigo todos los bienes y efectos qe. posean.

Art. III.

Para la execucion del articulo antecedente se nombrarán por cada una de las dos Altas Partes contratantes un Comisario y un Geometra qe. se juntarán en Natchez en la orilla izquierda del Misisipi antes de expirar el termino de seis meses despues de la ratificacion de la convencion presente, y procederán à la demarcacion de estos limites conforme à lo estipulado en el articulo anterior. Levantarán planos, y formarán Diarios de sus operaciones que se reputarán como parte de este Tratado, y tendran la misma fuerza que si estubieran insertas en el. Y si por qualquier motivo se creyese necesario que los dichos Comisarios y Geometras fuesen acompañados con Guardias, se les darán en numero igual por el General que mande las tropas de S. M. en las dos Floridas, y el Comandante de las tropas de los Estados Unidos en su territorio del sudoeste, que obrarán de acuerdo y amistosamente asi en este punto, como en el de apronto de viveres ê instrumentos, y en tomar qualesquiera otras disposiciones neccesarias para la execucion de

instruments and making every other arrangement which may be necessary or useful for the execution of this article.

Art. IV.

It is likewise agreed that the Western boundary of the United States which separates them from the Spanish Colony of Louissiana, is in the middle of the channel or bed of the River Missisippi from the Northern boundary of the said States to the completion of the thirty first degree of latitude North of the Equator; and his Catholic Majesty has likewise agreed that the navigation of the said River in its whole breadth from its source to the Ocean shall be free only to his Subjects, and the Citizens of the United States, unless he should extend this privilege to the Subjects of other Powers by special convention.

Art. V.

The two High contracting Parties shall by all the means in their power maintain peace and harmony among the several Indian Nations who inhabit the country adjacent to the lines and Rivers which by the preceding Articles form the boundaries of the two Floridas; and the beter to obtain this effect both Parties oblige themselves expressly to restrain by force all hostilities on the part of the Indian Nations living within their boundaries: so that Spain will not suffer her Indians to attack the citizens of the United States, nor the Indians inhabiting their territory; nor will

este articulo.

Art. IV.

Se han convenido igualmente que el Limite Occidental del territorio de los Estados Unidos qe. los separa de la Colonia Española de la Luisiana, está en medio del Canal ô Madre del Rio Misisipi, desde el limite septentrional de dichos Estados hasta el complemento de los treinta y un grados de latitud al Norte del Equador; y S. M. Catolica ha convenido igualmente en que la navegacion de dicho Rio en toda su extension desde su orilla hasta el Occeano, será libre solo â sus subditos, y á los Ciudadanos de los Estados Unidos, â menos que por algun tratado particular haga extensiva esta libertad à subditos de otras Potencias.

Art. V.

Las dos Altas Partes contratantes procurarán por todos los medios posibles mantener la paz, y buena armonía entre las diversas Naciones de Indios que habitan los terrenos adyacentes â las lineas y Rios que en los articulos anteriores forman los limites de las dos Floridas; y para conseguir mejor este fin se obligan expresamente ambas Potencias á reprimir con la fuerza todo genero de hostilidades de parte de las Naciones Indias que habitan dentro de la linea de sus respectivos limites: de modo que ni la España permitirá que sus Indios ataquen â los qe. vivan en el

the United States permit these last mentioned Indians to commence hostilities against the Subjects of his Catholic Majesty, or his Indians in any manner whatever.

And whereas treaties of Friendship exist between the two contracting Parties and the said Nations of Indians, it is hereby agreed that in future no treaty of alliance or other whatever (except treaties of Peace) shall be made by either Party with the Indians living within the boundary of the other; but both Parties will endeavour to make the advantages of the Indian trade common and mutualy beneficial to their respective Subjects and Citizens observing in all things the most complete reciprocity; so that both Parties may obtain the advantages arising from a good understanding with the said Nations, without being subject to the expence which they have hitherto occasioned.

Art. VI.

Each Party shall endeavour by all means in their power to protect and defend all Vessels and other effects belonging to the Citizens or Subjects of the other, which shall be within the extent of their jurisdiction by sea or by land, and shall use all their efforts to recover and cause to be restored to the right owners their Vessels and effects which may have been taken from them within the extent of their said jursidiction whether they are at war or not with the Power whose Subjects have

territorio de los Estados Unidos ô â sus ciudadanos; ni los Estados qe. los suyos hostilizen â los Subditos de S. M. Catolica ô â sus Indios de manera alguna.

Exîstiendo varios tratados de amistad entre las expresadas Naciones y las dos Potencias, se ha convenido en no hacer en lo venidero alianza alguna ô tratado (excepto los de Paz) con las Naciones de los Indios que habitan dentro de los limites de la otra parte; aunque procurarán hacer comun su comercio en beneficio amplio de los Subditos y Ciudadanos respectivos, guardandose en todo la reciprocidad mas completa: de suerte qe. sin los dispendios que han causado hasta ahora dichas Naciones á las dos Partes contratantes consigan ambas todas las ventajas qe. debe producir la armonía con ellas.

Art. VI.

Cada una de las dos Partes contratantes procurará por todos los medios posibles protexer y defender todos los Buques y qualesquiera otros efectos pertenecientes â los Subditos y Ciudadanos de la otra que se hallen en la extension de su jurisciccion por Mar ô por Tierra; y empleará todos sus esfuerzos para recobrar y hacer restituir â los Propietarios lexitimos los Buques y Efectos que se les hayan quitado en la extension de dicha jurisdiccion estén ô no en guerra con la Potencia cuyos subditos

taken possession of the said effects.

Art. VII.

And it is agreed that the Subjects or Citizens of each of the contracting Parties, their Vessels, or effects shall not be liable to any embargo or detention on the part of the other for any military expedition or other public or private purpose whatever; and in all cases of seizure, detention, or arrest for debts contracted or offences committed by any Citizen or Subject of the one Party within the jurisdiction of the other, the same shall be made and prosecuted by order and authority of law only and according to the regular course of proceedings usual in such cases. The Citizens and Subjects of both Parties shall be allowed to employ such Advocates, Sollicitors, Notaries, Agents, and Factors, as they may judje proper in all their affairs and in all their trials at law in which they may be concerned before the tribunals of the other Party, and such Agents shall have free access to be present at the proceedings in such causes, and at the taking of all examinations and evidence which may be exhibited in the said trials.

Art. VIII.

In case the Subjects and inhabitants of either Party with their shipping whether public and of war or private and of merchants be forced through stress of weather, pursuit of Pirates, or Enemis, or any other urgent necessity for seeking of shelter and harbor to retreat and enter into any of the

hayan interceptado dichos Efectos.

Art. VII.

Se ha convenido que los Ciudadanos y Subditos de una de las Partes contratantes, sus Buques, ô efectos no podran sugetarse â ningun embargo ô detencion de parte de la otra, â causa de alguna expedicion militar, uso publico, ô particular de qualquiera que sea; y en los casos de aprehension, detencion, ô arresto bien sea por deudas contrahidas û ofensas cometidas por algun Ciudadano ô Subdito de una de las Partes contratantes en la jurisdiccion de la otra, se procederá unicamente por orden y autoridad de la Justicia, y segun los tramites ordinarios seguidos en semejantes casos. Se permitira à los Ciudadanos y Subditos de ambas Partes emplear los Abogados, Procuradores, Notarios, Agentes, ô Factores que juzguen mas à proposito en todos sus asuntos y en todos los Pleytos qe. podrán tener en los Tribunales de la otra Parte, â los quales se permitirá igualmente el tener libre acceso en las causas, y estar presentes â todo exâmen y testimonios que podran ocurrir en los Pleytos.

Art. VIII.

Quando los Subditos y habitantes de la una de las dos Partes contratantes con sus Buques bien sean publicos y de guerra, bien particulares ô mercantiles se viesen obligados por una tempestad, por escapar de Piratas ô de Enemigos, ô por qualquiera otra necesidad urgente â buscar refugio y abrigo

Rivers, Bays, Roads, or Ports belonging to the other Party, they shall be received and treated with all humanity, and enjoy all favor, protection and help, and they shall be permitted to refresh and provide themselves at reasonable rates with victuals and all things needful for the sustenance of their persons or reparation of their Ships, and prosecution of their voyage; and they shall no ways be hindered from returning out of the said Ports, or Roads, but may remove and depart when and whither they please without any let or hindrance.

Art. IX.

All Ships and merchandize of what nature soever which shall be rescued out of the hands of any Pirates or Robbers on the high seas shall be brought into some Port of either State and shall be delivered to the custody of the Officers of that Port in order to be taken care of and restored entire to the true proprietor as soon as due and sufficient proof shall be made concerning the property there of.

Art. X.

When any Vessel of either Party shall be wrecked, foundered, or otherwise damaged on the coasts or within the dominion of the other, their respective Subjects or Citizens shall receive as well for themselves as for their Vessels and effects the same assistence which would be due to the inhabitants of the Country where the damage happens, and shall pay the same

en alguno de los Rios, Bahias, Radas, ô Puertos de una de las dos Partes, serán recibidos, y tratados con humanidad, y gozaran de todo fabor, proteccion y socorro, y les será licito proveerse de refrescos, viveres y demas cosas ncecsarias para su sustento, para componer los Buques, y continuar su viaje, todo mediante un precio equitativo; y no se les detendrá ô impedirá de modo alguno el salir de dichos Puertos ô Radas, antes bien podran retirarse y partir como y quando les pareciere sin ningun obstaculo ô impedimento.

Art. IX.

Todos los Buques y mercaderias de qualquiera naturaleza que sean que se hubiesen quitado à algunos Piratas en Alta Mar, y se traxesen à algun Puerto de una de las dos Potencias, se entregarán alli â los Oficiales ô Empleados en dicho Puerto â fin de que los guarden y restituyan integramente â su verdadero propietario luego que hiciese constar debida y plenamente que era su legitima propiedad.

Art. X.

En el caso de que un Buque perteneciente à una de las dos Partes contratantes naufragase, varase, ô sufriese alguna avería en las Costas ô en los dominios de la otra, se socorrerá â los Subditos ô Ciudadanos respectivos, asi â sus personas, como â sus Buques y efectos, del mismo modo que se haría con los habitantes del Pais donde suceda la desgracia, y pagaran solo las mis-

charges and dues only as the said inhabitants would be subject to pay in a like case: and if the operations of repair should require that the whole or any part of the cargo be unladen, they shall pay no duties, charges, or fees on the part which they shall relade and carry away.

Art. XI.

The Citizens and Subjects of each Party shall have power to dispose of their personal goods within the jurisdiction of the other by testament, donation, or otherwise; and their representatives being Subjects or Citizens of the other Party shall succeed to their said personal goods, whether by testament or ab intestato and they may take possession thereof either by themselves or others acting for them, and dispose of the same at their will paying such dues only as the inhabitants of the Country wherein the said goods are shall be subject to pay in like cases, and in case of the absence of the representatives, such care shall be taken of the said goods as would be taken of the goods of a native in like case, until the lawful owner may take measures for receiving them. And if question shall arise among several claimants to which of them the said goods belong the same shall be decided finally by the laws and Judges of the Land wherein the said goods are. And where on the death of any person holding real estate within the territories of the one Party, such real estate would by the laws

mas cargas y derechos qe. se hubieran exîgido de dichos habitantes en semejante caso, y si fuese necesario para componer el Buque qe. se descargue el cargamento en todo ô en parte, no pagarán impuesto alguno, carga, ô derecho de lo que se buelva â embarcar para ser exportado.

Art. XI.

Los Ciudadanos ô Subditos de una de las dos Partes contratantes, tendran en los Estados de la otra la libertad de disponer de sus bienes personales bien sea por testamento, donacion, û otra manera, y si sus herederos fuesen Subditos ô Ciudadanos de la otra Parte contratante, sucederán en sus bienes ya sea en virtud de testamento ô ab intestato y podran tomar posesion bien en persona ô por medio de otros que hagan sus veces, y disponer como les pareciere sin pagar mas derechos que aquellos qe. deben pagar en semejante caso los habitantes del Pais donde se verificase la herencia. Y si estubiesen ausentes los herederos se cuydará de los bienes que les hubiesen tocado, del mismo modo que se hubiera hecho en semejante ocasion con los bienes de los naturales del Pais, hasta que el legitimo Propietario haya aprobado las disposiciones para recoger la herencia. Si se Suscitasen disputas entre diferentes competidores que tengan derecho â la herencia, seran determinadas en ultima instancia segun las leyes y por los Jueces del Pais en que vacase la herencia. Y si por la muerte

of the Land descend on a Citizen or Subject of the other were he not disqualified by being an alien, such subject shall be allowed a reasonable time to sell the same and to withdraw the proceeds without molestation, and exempt from all rights of detraction on the part of the Government of the respective states.

Art. XII.
The merchant Ships of either of the Parties which shall be making into a Port belonging to the enemy of other Party and concerning whose voyage and the species of goods on board her there shall be just grounds of suspicion shall be obliged to exhibit as well upon the high seas as in the Ports and havens not only her passports but likewise certificates expressly shewing that her goods are not of the number of those which have been prohibited as contraband.

Art. XIII.
For the beter promoting of commerce on both sides, it is agreed that if a war shall break out between the said two Nations one year after the proclamation of war shall be allowed to the merchants in the Cities and Towns where they shall live for collecting and transporting their goods and merchandizes, and if any thing be taken from them, or any injury be done them within that term by either Party, or the People or Subjects of

de alguna persona que poseyese bienes raizes sobre el territorio de una de las Partes contratantes, estos bienes raizes llegasen â pasar segun las leyes del Pais â un Subdito ô Ciudadano de la otra Parte, y este por su calidad de extrangero fuese inhabil para poseerlos, obtendra un termino conveniente para venderlos y recoger su producto, sin obstaculo, exento de todo derecho de retencion de parte del Gobierno de los Estados respectivos.

Art. XII.
A los Buques mercantes de las dos Partes qe. fuesen destinados â Puertos pertenecientes â una Potencia enemiga de una de las dos, cuyo viage y naturaleza del cargamento diese justas sospechas, se les obligará à presentar bien sea en alta Mar bien en los Puertos y Cabos no solo sus pasaportes sino tambien los certificados que probarán expresamente que su cargamento no es de la especie de los que están prohibidos como de contrabando.

Art. XIII.
A fin de faborecer el comercio de ambas Partes se ha convenido que en el caso de romperse la guerra entre las dos Naciones, se concedera el termino de un año despues de su declaracion á los Comerciantes en las Villas y Ciudades que habitan, para juntar y transportar sus mercaderias, y si se les quitase alguna parte de ellas ô hiciese algun daño durante el tiempo prescrito arria por una de las dos Potencias, sus Pueblos ô Subditos, se

either, full satisfaction shall be made for the same by the Government.

Art. XIV.
No subject of his Catholic Majesty shall apply for or take any commission or letters of marque for arming any Ship or Ships to act as Privateers against the said United States or against the Citizens, People or inhabitants of the said United States, or against the property of any of the inhabitants of any of them, from any Prince or State with which the said United States shall be at war.

Nor shall any Citizen, Subject or Inhabitant of the said United States apply for or take any commission or letters of marque for arming any Ship or Ships to act as Privateers against the subjects of his Catholic Majesty or the property of any of them from any Prince or State with which the said King shall be at war. And if any person of either Nation shall take such commissions or letters of marque he shall be punished as a Pirate.

Art. XV.
It shall be lawful for all and singular the Subjects of his Catholic Mayesty, and the Citizens People, and inhabitants of the said United States to sail with their Ships with all manner of liberty and security, no distinction being made who are the proprietors of the merchandizes laden thereon from any Port to the Places of those who now are or hereafter shall be at enmity with his Catholic Majesty or the United

les dará en este punto entera satisfaccion por el Gobierno.

Art. XIV.
Ningun Subdito de S. M. Catolica tomará encargo ô patente para armar Buque ô Buques qe. obren como Corsarios contra dichos Estados Unidos, ô contra los Ciudadanos, Pueblos, y habitantes de los mismos, ô contra su propiedad ô la de los habitantes de alguno de ellos de qualquier Principe que sea con quien estubieren en guerra los Estados Unidos.

Igualmente ningun Ciudadano ô habitante de dichos Estados Unidos pedirá ô acceptará encargo ô patente para armar algun Buque ô Buques con el fin de perseguir los Subditos de S. M. Catolica, ô apoderarse de su propiedad, de qualquier Principe ô Estado que sea con quien estubiese en guerra S. M. Catolica. Y si algun individuo de una ô de otra Nacion tomase semejantes encargos ô patentes sera castigado como Pirata.

Art. XV.
Se permitirá à todos y â cada uno de los Subditos de S. M. Catolica; y â los Ciudadanos Pueblos y habitantes de dichos Estados qe. puedan navegar con sus Embarcaciones con toda libertad y seguridad, sin que haya la menor excepcion por este respeto aunque los propietarios de las mercanderias cargadas en las referidas embarcaciones vengan del Puerto que quieran y las traygan destinadas â qual-

States. It shall be likewise lawful for the Subjects and inhabitants aforesaid to sail with the Ships and merchandizes aforementioned, and to trade with the same liberty and security from the Places, Ports, and Havens of those who are Enemies of both or either Party without any opposition or distrubance whatsoever, not only directly from the Places of the Enemy aforementioned to neutral Places but also from one Place belonging to an Enemy to another Place belonging to an Enemy, whether they be under the jurisdiction of the same Prince or under several, and it is hereby stipulated that Free Ships shall also give freedom to goods, and that every thing shall be deemed free and exempt which shall be found on board the Ships belonging to the Subjects of either of the contracting Parties although the whole lading or any part thereof should appartain to the Enemies of either; contraband goods being always excepted. It is also agreed that the same liberty be extended to persons who are on board a free Ship, so that, although they be Enemies to either Party they shall not be made Prisoners or taken out of that free Ship unless they are Soldiers and in actual service of the Enemies.

quiera Plaza de una Potencia actualmente enemiga ô qe. lo sea despues asi de S. M. Catolica como de los Estados Unidos. Se permitirá igualmente à dos Subditos y habitantes mencionados navegar con sus Buques y mercaderias, y frequëntar con igual liberatad y seguridad las Plazas y Puertos de las Potencias enemigas de las Partes contratantes ô de una de ellas sin oposicion û obstaculo, y de comerciar no solo desde los puertos del dicho enemigo à un Puerto neutro directamente, sino tambien desde uno enemigo â otro tal bien se encuentre bajo su jurisdicion ô bajo la de muchos; y se estipula tambien por el presente tratado que los Buques libres asegurarán igualmente la libertad de las mercaderias, y que se juzgaran libres todos los efectos que se hallasen â bordo de los Buques que pereneciesen â los Subditos de una de las Partes contratantes, aun quando el cargamento, por entero ô parte de el fuese de los enemigos de una de las dos; bien entendido sin embargo qe. el contrabando se exceptua siempre. Şe ha convenido asimismo que la propia libertad gozarán los sugetos que pudiesen encontrarse â bordo del Buque libre aun quando fuesen enemigos de una de las dos Partes contratantes, y por lo tanto no se les podra hacer Prisioneros ni separarlos de dichos Buques, â menos qe. no tengan la qualidad de Militares, y esto hallandose en aquella sazon empleados en el servicio del enemigo.

Art. XVI.

This liberty of navigation and commerce shall extend to all kinds of merchandizes excepting those only which are distinguished by the name of contraband; and under this name of contraband or prohibited goods shall be comprehended arms, great guns, bombs, with the fusees, and other things belonging to them, cannon ball, gun powder, match, pikes, swords, lances, speards, halberds, mortars, petards, granades, salpetre, muskets, musket ball bucklers, helmets, breast plates, coats of mail, and the like kind of arms proper for arming soldiers, musket rests, belts, horses with their furniture and all other warlike instruments whatever. These merchandizes which follows shall not be reckoned among contraband or prohibited goods; that is to say, all sorts of cloths and all other manufactures woven of any wool, flax, silk, cotton, or any other materials whatever, all kinds of wearing aparel together with all species whereof they are used to be made, gold and silver as well coined as uncoined, tin, iron, latton, copper, brass, coals, as also wheat, barley, oats, and any other kind of corn and pulse: tobacco and likewise all manner of spices, salted and smoked flesh, salted fish, cheese and butter, beer, oils, wines, sugars, and all sorts of salts, and in general all provisions which serve for the sustenance of life. Furthermore all kinds of cotton, hemp,

Art. XVI.

Esta libertad de navegacion y de comercio debe extenderse â toda especie de mercaderias, exceptuando solo las que se comprehenden bajo el nombre de contrabando ô de mercaderias prohibidas: quales son las armas, cañones, bombas con sus mechas y demas cosas pertenecientes â lo mismo: balas, polvora, mechas, picas espadas, lanzas, dardos, alabardas, morteros, petardos, granadas, salitre, fusiles, balas escudos casquetes, corazas, cotas de malla, y otras armas de esta especie propias para armar â los Soldados. Portamosquetes, bandoleras, Caballos, con sus armas y otros instrumentos de guerra sean los que fueren. Pero los genros y mercaderias que se nombrarán ahora, no se comprehenderán entre los de contrabando ô cosas prohibidas: â saber, toda especie de paños y qualesquiera otras telas de lana, lino, Seda, algodon, û otras qualesquiera materias toda especie de vestidos con las telas de que se acostumbran hacer, el oro y la plata labrada en moneda ô no, el estaño yerro, laton, cobre, bronce, carbon, del mismo modo que la cevade, el trigo, la avena, y qualesquiera otro genero de legumbres: el tabaco y toda la especieria, carne salada y ahumada, pescado salado, queso y manteca, cerveza, aceytes, vinos, azucar y toda especie de sal, y en general todo genero de provisiones que sirven para el sustento de la vida. Ademas toda especie de

flax, tar, pitch, ropes, cables, sails, sail cloths, anchors, and any parts of anchors, also ship masts, planks, wood of all kind, and all other things proper either for building or repairing ships, and all other goods whatever which have not been worked into the form of any instrument prepared for war by land or by sea, shall not be reputed contraband, much less such as have been already wrought and made up for any other use: all which shall be wholly reckoned among free goods, as likewise all other merchandizes and things which are not comprehended and particularly mentioned in the foregoing enumeration of contraband goods: so that they may be transported and carried in the freest manner by the subjects of both parties, even to

such towns or Places being only excepted as are at that time besieged, blocked up, or invested. And except the cases in which any Ship of war or Squadron shall in consequence of storms or other accidents at sea be under the necessity of taking the cargo of any trading Vessel or Vessels, in which case they may stop the said Vessel or Vessels and furnish themselves with necessaries, giving a receipt in order that the Power to whom the said ship of war belongs may pay for the articles so taken according to the price thereof at the Port to which they may appear to have been destined by the Ship's papers: and the two contracting Parties

algodon cañamo, lino, alquitran, pez, cuerdas, cables, velas, telas para velas, ancoras y partes de que se componen, mastiles, tablas, maderas de todas especies, y qualesquiera otras cosas que sirvan para la construccion y reparacion de los Buques, y otras qualesquiera materias que no tienen la forma de un instrumento preparado para la guerra por tierro ô por mar no seran reputadas de contrabando, y menos las que estan ya preparadas para otros usos. Todas las cosas que se acaban de nombrar deben ser comprehendidas entre las mercaderias libres, lo mismo que todas las demas mercaderias y efectos que no estan comprehendidos y nombrados expresamente en la enumeracion de los generos de contrabando: de manera que podran ser transportados y conducidos con la mayor libertad por los Subditos de las dos Partes contratentes, á las Plazas enemigas, exceptuando sin embargo las qe. se hallasen en la actualidad sitiadas, bloqueadas ô embestidas. Y los casos en que algun Buque de Guerra, ô Esquadra que por efecto de avería û otras causas se halle en necesidad de tomar los efectos que conduzca el Buque ô Buques de comercio, pues en tal caso podra detenerlos para aprovisionarse y dar un recibo para que la Potencia cuyo sea el Buque tome los efectos, los pague segun el valor que tendrian en el Puerto adonde se dirigiese el propietario segun lo expresen sus cartas de navegacion: obligandose

engage that the Vessels shall not be detained longer than may be absolutely necessary for their said Ships to supply themselves with necessaries: that they will immediately pay the value of the receipts: and indemnify the proprietor for all losses which he may have sustained in consequence of such transaction.

Art. XVII.

To the end that all manner of dissentions and quarels may be avoided and prevented on one side and the other, it is agreed that in case either of the Parties hereto should be engaged in a war, the ships and Vessels belonging to the Subjects or People of the other Party must be furnished with sea letters or passports expressing the name, property, and bulk of the Ship, as also the name and place of habitation of the master or commander of the said Ship, that it may appear thereby that the Ship really and truly belongs to the Subjects of one of the Parties; which passport shall be made out and granted according to the form annexed to this Treaty. They shall likewise be recalled every year, that is, if the ship happens to return home within the space of a year. It is likewise agreed that such ships being laden, are to be provided not only with passports as above mentioned but also with certificates containing the several particulars of the cargo, the place whence the ship sailed, that so it may be known whether any forbidden or contraband goods be

las dos Partes contratantes â no detener los Buques mas de lo que sea absolutamente necesario para aprovisionarse, pagar inmediatamente los recibos, y â indemnizar todos los daños qe. sufra el propietario â consequencia de semejante suceso.

Art. XVII.

A fin de evitar entre ambas Partes toda especie de disputas y quejas, se ha convenido qe. en el caso de que una de las dos Potencias se hallase empeñada en una guerra, los Buques y Bastimentos pertenecientes à los Subditos ô Pueblos de la otra, deberan llevar consigo patentes de Mar ô pasaportes que expresen el nombre, la propiedad, y el porte del Buque, como tambien el nombre y morada de su dueño y Comandante de dicho Buque, para que de este modo conste que pertenece real y verdaderamente â los Subditos de una de las dos Partes contratantes; y que dichos pasaportes deberan expedirse segun el modelo adjunto al presente tratado. Todos los años deberán renovarse estos pasaportes en el caso de que el Buque buelva â su Pais en el espacio de un año. Igualmente se ha convenido en que los Buques mencionados arriba si estubiesen cargados, deberán llevar no solo los pasaportes sino tambien certificados que contengan el pormenor del cargamento, el lugar de donde ha salido el Buque, y la declaracion de

on board the same; which certificates shall be made out by the Officers of the place whence the ship sailed in the accustomed form; and if any one shall think it fit or adviseable to express in the said certificates the person to whom the goods on board belong he may freely do so: without which requisites they may be sent to one of the Ports of the other contracting Party and adjudged by the competent tribunal according to what is above set forth, that all the circumstances of this omission having been well examined, they shall be adjudged to be legal prizes, unless they shall give legal satisfaction of their property by testimony entirely equivalent.

Art. XVIII.

If the Ships of the said subjects, People or inhabitants of either of the Parties shall be met with either sailing along the Coasts on the high Seas by any Ship of war of the other or by any Privateer, the said Ship of war or Privateer for the avoiding of any disorder shall remain out of cannon shot, and may send their boats aboard the merchant Ship which they shall so meet with, and may enter her to number of two or three men only to whom the master or Commander of such ship or vessel shall exhibit his passports concerning the property of the ship made out according to the form inserted in the present Treaty: and the ship when she shall have shewed such passports shall be free and at liberty to pursue her

las mercaderias de contrabando qe. pudiesen hallarse â bordo; cuyos certificados deberán expedirse en la forma acostumbrada por los Oficiales empleados en el Lugar de donde el Navio se hiciese â la vela; y si se juzgase util y prudente expresar en dichos pasaportes la persona propietaria de las mercaderias se podra hacer libremente: sin cuyos requisitos sera conducido à uno de los Puertos de la Potencia respectiva y juzgado por el tribunal competente con arreglo â lo arriba dicho, para que exâminadas bien las circunstancias de su falta sea condenado por de buena presa si no satisfaciese legalmente con los testimonios equivalentes en un todo.

Art. XVIII.

Quando un Buque perteneciente â los dichos Subditos, Pueblos, y habitantes de una de las dos Partes fuese encontrado navegando â lo largo de la Costa ô en plena Mar por un Buque de Guerra de la otra, ô por un corsario, dicho Buque de guerra ô corsario â fin de evitar todo desorden se mantendrá fuera del tiro de cañon, y podra enviar su Chalupa â bordo del Buque mercante, hacer entrar en el dos ô tres hombres â los quales enseñará el Patron, ô Comandante del Buque sus pasaportes y demas documentos que deberan ser conformes â lo prevenido en el presente tratrado, y probará la propiedad del Buque: y despues de haber exhibido semejante pasaporte, y documentos, se les dejará seguir libremente su

voyage, so as it shall not be lawful to molest or give her chace in any manner or force her to quit her intended course.

Art. XIX.

Consuls shall be reciprocally established with the privileges and powers which those of the most favoured Nations enjoy in the Ports where their consuls reside, or are permitted to be.

Art. XX.

It is also agreed that the inhabitants of the territories of each Party shall respectively have free access to the Courts of Justice of the other, and they shall be permitted to prosecute suits for the recovery of their properties, the payment of their debts, and for obtaining satisfaction for the damages which they may have sustained, whether the persons whom they may sue be subjects or Citizens of the Country in which they may be found, or any other persons whatsoever who may have taken refuge therein; and the proceedings and sentences of the said Court shall be the same as if the contending parties had been subjects or Citizens of the said Country.

Art. XXI.

In order to terminate all differences on account of the losses sustained by the Citizens of the United States in consequence of their vessels and cargoes having been taken by the Subjects of his Catholic Majesty during the late war between Spain and France, it is agreed that all such cases shall be referred to

viage sin que les sea licito el molestarles ni procurar de modo alguno darle caza û obligarle à dejar el rumbo qe. seguía.

Art. XIX.

Se establecerán Consules reciprocamente con los privilegios y facultades que gozaren los de las Naciones mas faborecidas en los Puertos donde los tubieren estas ô les sea licito el tenerlos.

Art. XX.

Se ha convenido igualmente que los habitantes de los territorios de una y otra Parte respectivamente seran admitidos en los tribunales de Justicia de la otra Parte, y les sera permitido el entablar sus Pleytos para el recobro de sus propiedades, pago de sus deudas, y satisfaccion de los daños que hubieren recibido bien sean las personas contra las quales se quejasen Subditos ô Ciudadanos del Pais en el que se hallen, ô bien sean qualesquiera otros sugetos que se hayan refugiado alli; y los Pleytos y sentencias de dichos tribunales seran las mismas que hubieran sido en el caso de que las Partes litigantes fuesen Subditos ô Ciudadanos del mismo Pais.

Art. XXI.

A fin de concluir todas las disensiones sobre las perdidas que los Ciudadanos de los Estados Unidos hayan sufrido en sus Buques y cargamentos apresados por los Vasallos de S. M. Catolica durante la guerra que se acaba de finalizar entre España y Francia se ha convenido que todos estos casos se

the final decision of Commissioners to be appointed in the following manner. His Catholic Majesty shall name one Commissioner, and the President of the United States by and with the advice and consent of their Senate shall appoint another, and the said two Commissioners shall agree on the choice of a third, or if they cannot agree so they shall each propose one person, and of two names so proposed one shall be drawn by lot in the presence of the two original Commissioners, and the person whose name shall be so drawn shall be the third Commissioner, and the three Commissioners so appointed shall be sworn impartially to examine and decide the claims in question according to the merits of the several cases, and to justice, equity, and the laws of Nations. The said Commissioners shall meet and sit at Philadelphia and in the case of the death, sickness, or necessary absence of any such commissioner his place shall be supplied in the same manner as he was first appointed, and the new Commissioner shall take the same oaths, and do the same duties. They shall receive all complaints and applications, authorized by this article during eighteen months from the day on which they shall assemble. They shall have power to examine all such persons as come before them on oath or affirmation touching the complaints in question, and also to receive in evidence all written testimony authenticated in such manner as they

determinarán finalmente por Comisarios que se nombrarán de esta manera. S. M. Catolica nombrará uno, y el Presidente de los Estados Unidos otro con consentimiento y aprobacion del Senado, y estos dos Comisarios nombrarán un tercero de comun acuerdo: pero si no pudiesen acordase cada uno nombrará una persona, y sus dos nombres puestos en suerte se sacarán en presencia de los dos Comisarios, resultando por tercero aquel cuyo nombre hubiese salido el primero. Nombrados asi estos tres Comisarios, jurarán que exâminarán y decidirán con inparcialidad las quejas de que se trata segun el merito de la diferencia de los casos, y segun dicten la justicia, equidad, y derecho de gentes. Dichos Comisarios se juntarán y tendran sus sesiones en Filadelfia, y en caso de muerte, enfermedad, ô ausencia precisa se reemplazará su plaza de la misma manera que se eligió, y el nuevo Comisario hará igual juramento y exercerá iguales funciones. En el termino de diez y ocho meses contados desde el dia en que se junten, admitirán todas las quejas y reclamaciones autorizadas por este articulo. Asimismo tendran autoridad para exâminar baxo la sancion del juramento â todas las personas que ocurran ante ellos sobre puntos relativos â dichas quejas, y recibirán como evidente todo testimonio escrito que de tal manera sea autentico que ellos lo juzguen digno de pedirle ô admitirle. La decision de dichos

shall think proper to require or admit. The award of the said Commissioners or any two of them shall be final and conclusive both as to the justice of the claim and the amount of the sum to be paid to the claimants; and his Catholic Majesty undertakes to cause the same to be paid in specie without deduction, at such times and Places and under such conditions as shall be awarded by the said Commissioners.

Art. XXII.

The two high contracting Parties hopping that the good correspondence and friendship which happily reigns between them will be further increased by this Treaty and that it will contribute to augment their prosperity and opulence, will in future give to their mutual commerce all the extension and favor which the advantage of both Countries may require; and in consequence of the stipulations contained in the IV. article his Catholic Majesty will permit the Citizens of the United States for the space of three years from this time to deposit their merchandize and effects in the Port of New Orleans, and to export them from thence without paying any other duty than a fair price for the hire of the stores, and his Majesty promises either to continue this permission if he finds during that time that it is not prejudicial to the interests of Spain, or if he should not agree to continue it there, he will assign to them on another part of the banks of the Missis-

Comisarios ô de dos de ellos sera final y concluyente tanto por lo qe. toca â la justicia de la queja como por lo que monte la suma que se deba satisfacer â los demandantes, y S. M. Catolica se obliga â hacer las pagar en especie sin rebaxa, y en las epocas lugares, y baxo las condiciones que se decidan por los Comisarios.

Art. XXII.

Esperando las dos Altas partes contratantes que la buena correspondencia y amistad que reyna actualmente entre si se estrechará mas y mas con el presente tratado, y que contribuirá à aumentar su prosperidad y opulencia, consederán reciprocamente en lo succesivo al comercio todas las ampliaciones ô fabores que exîgiese la utilidad de los dos Paises; y desde luego à consequencia de lo estipulado en el articulo IV. permitirá S. M. Catolica por espacio de tres años â los Ciudadanos de los Estados Unidos que depositen sus mercaderias y efectos en el Puerto de Nueva Orleans, y que las extraigan sin pagar mas derechos qe. un precio justo por el alquiler de los Almacenes ofreciendo S. M. continuar el termino de esta gracia si se experimentase durante aquel tiempo que no es perjudicial â los intereses de la España, ó sino conviniese su continuacion en aquel Puerto proporcionará en otra parte de las orillas del Rio Misisipi un igual establecimiento.

sipi an equivalent establishment.

Art. XXIII.

The present Treaty shall not be in force until ratified by the Contracting Parties, and the ratifications shall be exchanged in six months from this time, or sooner if possible.

In Witness whereof We the underwritten Plenipotentiaries of His Catholic Majesty and of the United States of America have signed this present Treaty of Friendship, Limits and Navigation and have thereunto affixed our seals respectively.

Done at San Lorenzo el Real this seven and twenty day of October one thousand seven hundred and ninety five.

(Seal) Thomas Pinckney
(Seal) El Principe de la Paz.

Art. XXIII.

El presente tratado no tendrá efecto hasta que las Partes contratantes le hayan ratificado, y las ratificaciones se cambiarán en el termino de seis meses, ô antes si fuese posible contando desde este dia.

En fe de lo qual Nosotros los infraescritos Plenipotenciarios de S. M. Catolica y de los Estados Unidos de America hemos firmado en virtud de nuestros plenos poderes este tratado de Amistad, Limites, y Navegacion, y le hemos puesto nuestros sellos respectivos.

Hecho en San Lorenzo el Real à veinte y siete de Octubre de mil setecientos noventa y cinco.

(Seal) Thomas Pinckney
(Seal) El Principe de la Paz.

Tariff Schedule
of 1796

"A tariff, agreed upon by the merchants from the Province of Louisiana, as a consequence of and for the observance throughout the Province as decreed by His majesty by Royal Order of 24 May 1796, the General Office of Royal Revenue of this City and the rest of the Province shall conform thereto in the collection of royal duties which shall be paid on merchandise and imported goods obtained from foreign ports under the rules set forth in the Royal Order of 9 July 1793," as posted by Juan Ventura Morales, 24 August 1796. The full tariff with accompanying note is located in the Archivo General de Indias (Sevilla), Papeles procedentes de la Isla de Cuba, legajo 184-A.

The tariff duty was based upon a determined value in minted silver reales, a coin whose value varied according to its actual silver content. Generally minted in Mexico, the real was used extensively throughout the Western Hemisphere. The Mexican peso, used interchangeably with the American dollar and the piastre with regard to purchasing power, was worth eight reales. Thus, each real was worth about 12½ cents. J. Villasana Haggard, *Handbook for Translators of Spanish Historical Documents* (Austin, 1941), 106, values the peso in use in Louisiana at the close of the eighteenth century at approximately $1.7151 (using the American dollar for 1936 as his standard).

Appendix II

In addition to the currency values, the standards of weights and measures varied also. The following are referred to in the text of the document: (1) Ana: a unit for the measurement of cloth (English "ell"), equal to about forty-five inches; (2) Barrica: a "cask" containing about sixty gallons of liquid; (3) Barrel: a unit of measurement that was not standardized as to weight, but which referred both to volume (as measured in gallons from 25 to 32), and also to weight (from 180 to 260 English pounds); (4) Quintal: equaled a unit of weight that varied, the Mexican quintal contained 101.44 pounds; and (5) La Velte: an obsolete French unit of measurement equal to seven English quarts. The final determination of values, breakage, and other matters pertaining to the amount of tariff owed on goods imported or exported by merchants was determined by the intendant and his staff, who had a substantial amount of flexibility in such matters.

The import duties which follow are part of the general tariff schedule prepared by Morales in 1796. Throughout the *Observations*, Pitot stresses the importance of imports for the commerce in Louisiana. The amount of the duty is listed in minted silver reales. Eight reales equal approximately one American dollar.

ITEM	TARIFF IN MINTED SILVER REALES
Boxed fans, bone and ivory, at a 10 percent increase over invoice	
Fans, wood. See Notions	
Steel, in bars, from all possessions	80
Cooking oil, per a dozen bottles	32
Linseed [linaza] oil, per gallon	5
Ordinary oil, per dozen bottles	12
Fish oil, per gallon	2½
Olives, per dozen jars	16
Olives, per jug	6
Ginger, per quintal	56
Queen of Hungary medicinal water, per dozen vials	12
Medicine Water (Our Lady of Carmel), per dozen vials	12

ITEM	TARIFF IN MINTED SILVER REALES
Eau de toilette, all kinds, per bottle	3
Brandy, per dozen bottles	16
Brandy, from Bordeaux, in small barrels	18
Brandy, from Provence, in small barrels	12
Brandy, from Bordeaux, in casks, per velte	8
Brandy, from Provence, in casks, per velte	5
Rum, per cask	80
Whiskey, per gallon	3
Cherry Brandy, per dozen bottles	16
Alabaster, at a 10 percent increase over invoice	
Copper or brass wire, per quintal	200
White lead (Ceruse), per quintal	64
Capers, small and large; dozen flasks	18
Copperas, blue, white and green; quintal	32
Rugs, wool or worsted, per ana in squares	20
Jewelry: pearls, diamonds, and other fine stones, at 10 percent increase over invoice	
Red ochre, quintal	24
Massicot or litharge [lead monoxide for glazing], per quintal	50
Almonds, in husk; quintal	50
Almonds, husked; quintal	120
Starch, quintal	50
Birdseed, quintal	48
Alum, from all regions, quintal	48
Anchovies, dozen flasks	18
Anchovies, barrel of 180 lbs	80
Aniseed, quintal	40
Anisette, special quality, basket with two flasks	12
Anisette, ordinary quality, basket with two flasks	8
Chrystal chandeliers; 10 percent increase over invoice	
Herring and small fish, quintal	24
Leather harnesses with iron and copper buckles, for coaches, gigs, coupes, and other carriages; assorted pair or that necessary for three horses. For one or two horses prorated	200

ITEM	TARIFF IN MINTED SILVER REALES
Leather harnesses, with silver plated copper; assorted pair as in the foregoing	280
Tuna, dozen small flasks	24
Tuna, quintal	72
Hazelnuts (or filberts), quintal	28
Low, flat baskets oats, quintal; or trays, assorted qualities, 10 percent increase over invoice	
Latten, bras or similar alloy, quintal	200
Refined sugar, quintal	64
Sugar, in loaves, quintal	120
Sugar, in pieces, quintal	52
Brown sugar, quintal	52
Coarse brown sugar, quintal	40
Powdered sulphur, quintal	50
Sulphur in bricks, quintal	31
Prussian blue, quintal	1600
Spades or hoes, as finished ironwork tools, quintal	100
Codfish, quintal	32
White cotton cloth. See Cotton cloth.	
Lead bullets, quintal	50
Sheepskin, dressed; dozen	24
Ramrods, each	16
Waterproof cape, assorted: ½ to ¾ ana wide, each ana	4
Assorted batiste (fine cambric), the bolt or bundle of six anas	64
Batiste rough; bolt of 12 anas	80
Calfskin, dozen	64
Vermillion. See Cinnabar.	
Painted linen folding screens; each	96
Same of paper; each	48
Bidets, wooden; each	14
Biscuits, ordinary, quintal	32
Biscuits, fine, Quintal	48
Silk lace of all types, 10 percent increase over invoice	
Assorted linen bombazines, the ana	4

ITEM	TARIFF IN MINTED SILVER REALES
Fancy regular leather boots, the pair	40
Boots, ready to finish, the pair	16
Stockings, ready to finish	28
Short stockings, ready to finish, and others	10
Empty bottles, per 100	36
Fine gold thread buttons, ounce	10
Fine silver thread buttons, ounce	8
Gold and silver brocade, over satin, Grode tour, taffeta and other silk materials, 10 percent increase over invoice	
Drinking jugs [Búcaros], the quintal	200
Lace trimmings, batiste, mouselline, and others, at 10 percent increase over invoice	
Candles. See worked wax	
Casks and barrels, new, unassembled	6
Horse mackerel, barrel	24
Cables (thick rope), quintal	60
Cocoa (chocolate), quintal	100
Coffee, quintal	96
Limestone, barrel	6
Mottled fabric, some with silk or mixed cloth of other types, all widths, qualities and colors; the ana	4
Assorted material [Calancanes] genuine and imitations; bolt of 12 anas	48
Two-wheeled calashes. See carriages	
Light chaises or gigs, utility, with necessary rigging, each	800
Assorted hose, dozen	40
Long buckskin trousers, pair	40
Short buckskin trousers, pair	24
Long pants of light canvas-like unbleached linen, the pair	4
Camel's hair cloth (fine wool), all colors, the ana	8
Same, but regular wool, all colors; the ana	4
Shirts of fine linen, trimmed with muslin or batiste; dozen	160
Shirts of coarse linen, trimmed with muslin or batiste; dozen	120
Shirts, but without trimming, dozen	80

Appendix II

ITEM	TARIFF IN MINTED SILVER REALES
Shirts, linen, for troops and hospitals; dozen	60
Shirts, striped or cotton gingham, assorted; dozen	48
Shirts, of light canvas, dozen	48
Shirts, of Silesian, laval, or Pontivi linen and for fencing, men or women	48
Cast bells and mortars, quintal	120
Cinnemon from Ceylon, quintal	1600
Chinese cinnamon, quintal	500
Gold and silver bugles for embroidery; ounce	32
Hemp, cleaned, quintal	44
Cane or rattan for walking sticks, 10 percent increase over invoice	
Writing quills, per thousand	48
Mahogany, from Santo Domingo, square foot	8
Carbines, good quality	200
Carbines, ordinary quality	60
Cloth [Carandali or Carandry] genuine, ordinary; bolt of ten to twelve anas	80
Cloth, but extra fine quality; bolt of 12 anas	120
Cloth, but imitation, bolt of 12 anas	56
Lump coal, cask	8
Cards, for cotton, pair	3
Parris green or verdigris, quintal	200
Tortoise-shell, quintal	1200
Carved tortoise-shell, quintal	2400
Carmine, fine quality, quintal	3000
Ordinary carmine, quintal	1500
Beef, barrel	60
Salt pork, barrel	80
Cardboard, quintal	50
Pasteboard, quintal	32
Chestnuts, quintal	30
Small boxes of assorted paints, at 10 percent over invoice	
Barley, quintal	28
Onions, quintal	12

ITEM	TARIFF IN MINTED SILVER REALES
Yellow paste wax, quintal	180
Formed yellow wax, quintal	250
White shaped wax, quintal	350
White paste wax, quintal	280
English aie, cask	64
English ale, in bottles, dozen	12
Beer from Holland, Flanders or other dominions, cask	48
Beer, the same as above, but per dozen bottles	10
Shoemaker's wax, quintal	100
Golden epaulets for officer's insignias, per ounce	16
Same as above of silver, per ounce	12
Cordovan slippers for ladies and gentlemen, the pair	6
Chocolate with sugar and cinnamon, quintal	400
Plain chocolate without sugar or cinnamon. See chocolate paste	
Waistcoats of gold or silver tissue, taffeta, satin and other fabrics or linens, striped or embroidered finished or unfinished; at 10 percent increase over invoice	
Glass shades or cylinders for candles, 10 percent increase over invoice	
Cinnabar or vermillion, quintal	600
Silk ribbon, all qualities, colors and origin, size 7 to 12, per bolt of 12 anas	10
Same as above, size 3 to 6, bolt of 12 anas	5
French silk ribbon, all colors, size 3 to 9, or others of similar quality, from another land, bolt of 60 anas	22
Black silk ribbon, assorted for dress trains, bolt of 12 anas	5
Satin-faced ribbon, wide, bolt of 12 anas	20
Same as above, but narrow width, bolt	10
Small ribbon, assorted, bolt of 60 anas	6
Skeins of woolen yarn, per piece	4½
Same as above of black linen thread, per piece size 2½ and 3, per dozen spools	20
Same as above of silk, with silver or gold embroidery, at 10 percent increase over invoice	
Velvet ribbons, about two inches wide, roll of 24 anas	72

ITEM	TARIFF IN MINTED SILVER REALES
Velvet ribbons, medium or narrow width, roll of 24 anas	16
Silk belts, embroidered or with gold or silver braided trimming, at 10 percent over invoice	
Leather belts, each	8
Church candles. See worked wax	
Prunes and raisins, per quintal	50
Nails of assorted sizes, per quintal	60
Cloves, the spice, per quintal	1600
Horsehair, per quintal	172
Cast copper, per quintal	280
Sheet copper, per quintal	200
Carriages, coupes, landaus, and other four-wheel carriages with their respective harnesses each	3200
Coffers and empty trunks, assorted, each	20
Strong English glue, per quintal	120
Same as above from Holland, Flanders, and other places, per quintal	100
Fish glue, per quintal	72
Double bed spreads, plush silk, each	120
Same as above of linen and woolen fabric, variegated and assorted, each	56
Same as above of calico or chintz, printed or flowered, quilted for double beds, likewise assorted, each	72
White cotton double bedspreads, each	48
Chinese double bedspreads, assorted, each	96
Pickled cabbage, quintal	20
Large elephant tusks, quintal	800
Same as above, but smaller, per quintal	400
Resin, quintal	40
Fine colors in powder for painting, not mentioned in this current tariff, per quintal	1600
Cumins, quintal	75
Wild or uncultivated cumins, quintal	50
Mother of pearl shells, fine quality, quintal	250
Same as above, ordinary quality, per quintal	64

ITEM	TARIFF IN MINTED SILVER REALES
Assorted dried sweetmeats, quintal	150
Same in preserves, quintal	100
Neckties of muslin, cambric or batiste, embroidered fancy or plain, per dozen	48
Neckties, assorted plain, dotted or striped, fancy or plain, dozen	36
Cork, quintal	40
Morocco leather, per dozen pieces	40
Fancy gold cord, 10 percent increase over invoice	
Same, but silver, same rate	
Same, but silk with gold and silver, at same rate	
Same, but woolen, per pound	16
Penknives. See hardware	
White Russian mattress ticking, wide, bolt of 29 to 30 anas	100
Same, but narrow, same size bolt	80
Mattress ticking, striped, blue, red or other assorted colors, two anas wide, per ana	14
Same, but 1¾ ana wide, per ana	12
Same, but 1½ ana wide, per ana	10
Same, but 1¼ ana wide, per ana	8
Same, but 1 ana wide, per ana	7
Same, but ⅞ ana wide, per ana	5
Same, but ¾ ana wide, per ana	4
Same, but ⅝ ana wide, per ana	3½
Same, but ½ ana wide, per ana	2½
Silk ticking mixed with cotton, assorted, ana	4
Striped, floral or bright red privit calico, ⅞ ana wide, per ana	6
Same, but ⁶/₈ ana wide, per ana	5
Same, but ⅝ ana wide, per ana	4½
Same, but ½ ana wide, per ana	3
Blue striped, floral or pattern calico, fancy, extra fancy and plain, ⅞ ana wide, per ana	4
Same, but ⁶/₈ ana wide, per ana	3
Same, but ⅝ ana wide, per ana	2½
Same, but ½ ana wide, per ana	2

ITEM	TARIFF IN MINTED SILVER REALES
White cotton goods, ⅞ ana, fine fancy and plain, per ana	4
Same, but ¾, ⅝, ⅔ ana, plain and extra quality, per ana	3
Dimity of corded cotton, fine white quality from Haarlem, ⁶/₈ to ⅞ ana wide, per ana	11
Same, but plain and extra, ⅝ and ⅔ ana wide, per ana	6
Same, fine quality, measuring ½, ⅝ and ⅔ anas wide, per ana	8
Dimity from Haarlem, fine and plain, per ana	5
Dimity, white, striped or solid from Flanders, England, Germany, and other lands; fine quality ⁶/₈ and ⅞ anas wide, per ana	9
Dimity, fine and fancy, per ana	9
Same, fine, ½, ⅝, and ⅔ anas wide, per ana	9
Same, fancy and plain, per ana	9
Dimity, buff-colored, and other colors, fancy ⁶/₈ and ⅞ ana wide, per ana	12
Same, but plain and special, per ana	7
Same, special, of ½, ⅝, and ⅔ anas wide, per ana	8
Quilted white dimity, fine ⁶/₈ and ⅞ anas wide, per ana	13
Same, but plain of same width, per ana	8
White dimity, fine quality, same widths, per ana	9
Same, but plain and extra qualities, same width, per ana	6
Blown crystal, at 10 percent increase over invoice	
Dimities, called Demites, per bolt of 9 to 10 anas	12
Tanned leathers, each	16
Rawhides, each	8
Dressed leather, per quintal	150
Leather tooled in gold or silver, at 10 percent increase over invoice	
Cured buffalo meat, per quintal	18
Chick-peas, shelled, per quintal	20
Caribbean sea turtle shells, unworked, per quintal	300
Buckets, leather, for fires, per dozen	100
Silk filosela damask, assorted, per ana	8
Dates, per quintal	100

ITEM	TARIFF IN MINTED SILVER REALES
Dressing gowns of silk, muslin, or linen, pattern cut, at 10 percent over invoice	
Drugs, basic or compound, all qualities and countries, same rate as above	
Rugs with cotton warp and wool filling, mixed, all lands, per ana	5
Staves for large barrels, per thousand	144
Ebony, per quintal	32
Gold, silver and linen lace, 10 percent over invoice	
Oilcloth of all qualities of canvas, per ana	4
Double-barrel shotgun trimmed in silver	200
Same, but plain	120
Single-barrel shotgun, trimmed in silver	160
Same, but plain and extra	48
Swords and rapiers, 10 percent over invoice	
Trade-goods mirrors, plain and fancy, per gross	80
Mirrors, plain and fancy, 10 percent over invoice	
Ambergris candles, per quintal	400
Tin, per same quantity	64
Rattan, straw and bamboo mats, per square ana	8
Tree bark mats, per piece	2
Fine blazed buckram, or bocasi, per ana	1½
Hemp burlap, per quintal	24
Canvas burlap, the same quantity	30
Cases for mathematicians and others, at 10 percent over invoice	
Chenille, wool and linen mixture, per ana	4
Spaghetti and other kinds of pasta, per quintal	40
Artifical flowers, 10 percent over invoice	
Bottles and bottle cases, 10 percent over invoice	
Bridles, fine quality, 10 percent over invoice	
Trading doos bridles, per dozen	48
Brandied fruits, all kinds, per jar	2½
Army muskets, each	40
Trade muskets, each	20
Gold braid, fine, per ounce	20

ITEM	TARIFF IN MINTED SILVER REALES
Same of silver, per ounce	12
Imitation gold braid, per pound	6
Same, of imitation silver, per pound	4
Same of linen, assorted as to color, widths, and quality, per roll of 30 anas	6
Same of silk, assorted as the above, per roll of 30 anas	16
Chamois skins, per dozen	24
Chick-peas, per quintal	32
Silk collars. See silk	
Gold and silver embroidered collars, per ana	8
Assorted linen collars, per ana	2
Gin in casks, per gallon	4
Same in cases, per dozen bottles	20
Ginghams. See striped material	
Linen caps, per dozen	40
Same of cotton, per dozen	20
Same of silk, mixed with other assorted, per dozen	32
Same of wool, linen, cotton, and other cloth, assorted, per dozen	24
Small colored bonbons, per quintal	150
Cochineal, fancy, per quintal	2800
Same, but wild, ground up or in powder, per quintal	800
Chalk [or Fuller's earth], per quintal	8
Men's suede gloves, per dozen	36
Same, of kidskin, mixed, for men or women, per dozen	12
Lisle gloves, assorted, for men or women, per dozen	24
Same of cotton, assorted as the foregoing, per dozen	20
Same of beaverskin, for men or women, per dozen	72
Same of wool, assorted, per dozen	12
Gold and silver trimmings, for dresses and small swords, at 10 percent over invoice	
Blue ginghams, assorted, per bolt of 14 to 16 anas	56
Same, but imitation for the Indiana trade, bolt of 14 anas	36
Same, floral pattern, assorted, per bolt of 14 anas	56

ITEM	TARIFF IN MINTED SILVER REALES
Same, various qualities, blue and white stripes, ⅔ ana wide, per bolt of 3½ anas	10
Gingham, ¾ and ⅚ anas wide, assorted, per bolt of 5 to 6 anas	30
Beans, per quintal	13
Kidney beans, all qualities, per quintal	12
Flour, per barrel of 180 lbs.	48
Same fron Kentucky and the Ohio country, per barrel	32
Ironwork, such as locks, hinges, and latches, and miscellaneous iron work made to ornament windows, carriages, doors, and so on, per quintal	100
Wrought iron for gratings, balconies, hammers, cask stands, arch brackets, ungilded andirons, chains, shackles, hammers, anvils, crowbars, balance scales, and other basic ironwork, per quintal	72
Assorted iron bars, per quintal	36
Cast iron, such as pressing irons, kettles, andirons, and so on, per quintal	28
Figs, per quintal	50
Narrow ribbon. See white linen ribbon	
Pack-thread or hemp twine, per quintal	150
White thread from France, England, and other lands, per pound	9
Same, but assorted colors, per the same	8
Same, but of cotton, per the same	6
Rough thread from Rennes and others of like quality, per the same	3
Wire. See common hardware	
Copper wire. See under copper wire	
Gold and silver thread, per ounce	16
Imitation gold and silver threads. See dry goods	
Blades for small swords, savers, knives and machetes, 10 percent increase over invoice	
Sheets of tin from Germany, Spain and other lands, assorted, per 100	50
Cast tin, at 10 percent increase over invoice	
Panes of horn for lamps. See dry goods	

ITEM	TARIFF IN MINTED SILVER REALES
Hammered iron, per quintal	64
Cambric. See linen	
Cambric or linen batiste, plain and extra smooth, from Arras, Bapaume, Vervins, Scotland and other lands, all widths, per bolt of 15 anas	88
Ordinary linen or cambric, per bolt of 15 anas	56
Same as above, but striped or printed, fancy and extra quality, all widths, per bolt of 15 anas	120
Same as above, but plain, per bolt of 15 anas	64
Brown Holland [Holandillas or Sanealas fabric], per bolt of 12 anas	24
Fine linen cambric, assorted, per bolt of 12 to 14 anas	64
Batiste, look under its article	
Pitch or tar, per quintal	176
Axes and hatchets as wrought ironwork, per quintal	100
Corn meal, per barrel	14
Wide printed calico [indianas] from Provence and similar quality from elsewhere, per bolt of 10 anas	20
Narrow printed calico, narrow width, from the same, per bolt of 10 anas	12
Same from the West Indies, 10 percent over invoice	
Same from other lands, fancy quality, white and colored background, ¾ and ⅞ anas wide, per ana	7
Same but plain quality, per ana	4½
Same of ½, ⅝, and ⅔ anas wide, per ana	2½
Linen calico, from all lands, per ana	5
Same from Camayeux, or for upholstering, from everywhere, ¾ and greater widths, per ana	6
Same but ⅔ ana wide and less, per ana	3
Instruments for music, optics, astronomy, navigation, surgery and physics, at 10 percent over invoice	
All kinds of fruit jellies, per quintal	400
Ham, from everywhere, per quintal	80
Jasper, 10 percent over invoice	
Gems, 10 percent over invoice	

Tariff Schedule of 1796

ITEM	TARIFF IN MINTED SILVER REALES
Kirsch [Kirschwasser], per dozen bottles	32
Tiles, all sizes, quality, shapes, per thousand	24
Same for floors, all sizes, qualities and shapes, per thousand	48
Same of marble, per hundred	160
Lame of gold and silver from León, and other gold or silver cloth of equal quality, per ana	40

Wool and Woolen Material

ITEM	TARIFF
Assorted twilled woolens or serges, per ana	5
English baize for robes, per bolt of 30 anas, 10 percent over invoice	
100-thread baize, per bolt of 30 anas	150
Same, for bandages, per bolt of 28 to 29 anas	84
Same of white or colored wool or assorted flannels of various qualities, from ⅞ to 1¼ anas wide, per ana	7
Same, but ¾, ⅔, and ⅝ anas wide, fancy and extra quality, per ana	5
Same, same width, but plain quality, per ana	2½
Same, of 1 and 1½ anas wide, per ana	7
Blanket-cloth, or "Bergop-som," measuring ⅞, ¾, and ⅔ anas wide, per ana	4
"Bergop-som" or laced calmont, 1 and 1¼ anas wide, per ana	8
Same, but measuring ⅞, ½, and ⅔ anas wide, per ana	5
Assorted crepe, per ana	4
Calamandras or clalmancos, whatever width or type, per ana	3
Knitted "long Johns," per pair	10
Same, cutoffs, per pair	6
English Angora wool, and similar types, per bolt of 30 anas	150
Woolen capes, fancy and extra, each	160
Same, but plain, each	80
Same, but fancy trimmed in gold and silver braid, and lined with silk velvet, each	240
Gold carriage fabric from Flanders and elsewhere, per ana	14
Cashmere, from ½ and to ¾ anas wide, per ana	10
Damask, per ana	5
Glazed camlet, assorted, per ana	3

Appendix II

ITEM	TARIFF IN MINTED SILVER REALES
Assorted wool-like drugget, from England and elsewhere, per ana	6
Same of wool, stripped, patterned, or mottled, assorted, from everywhere, per ana	3½
English monkserge, and similar fabric, per ana	4

Notes

AUTHOR'S INTRODUCTION

1. The *Observations on Louisiana* were originally intended for publication in France, which James Pitot visited from August, 1802, to May, 1803. The discovery of the *Observations*, along with the pertinent addenda, is discussed by René J. Le Gardeur, Jr., and Henry C. Pitot in "An Unpublished Memoir of Spanish Louisiana, 1796–1802," in John Francis McDermott (ed.), *Frenchmen and French Ways in the Mississippi Valley* (Urbana, 1969). 73–86. A brief biography of James Pitot is that by Henry Clement Pitot, *James Pitot (1761– 1831): A Documentary Study* (New Orleans, 1968), which traces the subject's public and private life in detail. Grace King provides only a very cursory account in her *Creole Families of New Orleans* (New York, 1921), 429–30.
2. James Pitot was engaged in the sugar industry on the island of Saint-Domingue for ten years (1782–1792), and hence he was removed by his work from the literary circles and salons of Europe and America that were universally regarded as the centers of enlightenment, literature, and culture during this era. After his arrival in New Orleans in 1796, James Pitot became one of the leading merchants in the city. See John G. Clark, *New Orleans, 1718–1812: An Economic History* (Baton Rouge, 1970), 70.
3. The literature on Spanish Louisiana, 1762–1803, is voluminous; however, the most appropriate guides to the subject are: the bibliographical and chronological items provided by Jack D. L. Holmes, *A Guide to Spanish Louisiana 1762–1806* (New Orleans, 1970); and the series of essays on several subjects edited by John Francis McDermott, *The Spanish in the Mississippi Valley, 1762–1804* (Urbana, 1974). Among the several specialized studies of Louisiana under Spanish sovereignty, are the following classical studies by Arthur Preston Whitaker: *The Mississippi Question, 1795–1803: A Study in Trade, Politics, and Diplomacy* (New York, 1934); and *The Spanish-American Frontier, 1783–1795: The Westward Movement and the Spanish Retreat in the Mississippi Valley* (New York, 1927). A recent scholarly study that places Spain and Louisiana within the larger context of the competing powers is that by

Alexander de Conde, *This Affair of Louisiana* (New York, 1976), which provides a useful bibliography.

4. The retrocession of Louisiana by Spain to France was kept secret because the latter nation was at war with Great Britain, and British naval supremacy, as well as European entanglements concerning territorial changes in the Treaty of San Ildefonso (October 1, 1800), required it. See Arthur P. Whitaker, "Spain and the Retrocession of Louisiana," *American Historical Review*, XXXIX (1934), 454–76. The principal reason for preparing the *Observations on Louisiana* was to present the report to the French government, and thereby establish a business contact for the firm of Jean Lanthois and James Pitot, which they had founded in 1796.

5. By 1796 the influence of the French Revolution in Europe, America, and the French overseas possessions had already assumed many forms. One of the most important results in Saint-Domingue was that the black revolutionaries quoted the ideology of French thinkers in defense of the slave revolt. The most radical phase of the French Revolution, the Reign of Terror (1793–1794), had already run its course in France, but the legacy of revolutionary violence still manifested itself in the colonies for some time, so that Jacobins, the party of political violence, were suspected of hiding behind every tree ready to pounce upon legally constituted authorities. See the summary provided by Ernest R. Liljegren, "Jacobinism in Spanish Louisiana, 1792–1797," *Louisiana Historical Quarterly*, XXII (January, 1939), 47–97.

6. Pitot, *Documentary Study*, 41–42. The most scathing attack against Spanish influence in Louisiana was published in France in 1803 by Pierre Louis Berquin-Duvallon, *Vue de la colonie espagnole du Mississipi ou des provinces de Louisiane et Floride Occidentale en l'année 1802*. For a scholarly discussion of the same subject, see the analysis of the difficulties confronting Spanish administrators as described by Jack D. L. Holmes, "Some Economic Problems of Spanish Governors in Louisiana," *Hispanic American Historical Review*, XLII (November, 1962), 521–43.

7. James Pitot is very conscious here that being a critic of the Spanish government, a newcomer to Louisiana, and a Frenchman but with American citizenship, he is liable to immediate suspicion as one of the Jacobin sympathizers who still caused trouble. When he later visited France, Pitot never let on that he had become an American citizen at Philadelphia in 1796, "Passeport de et pour l'étranger, Jacques Pitot (an XI, 20 aôut 1802), série F 7, 10884 police générale, Archives Nationales de Paris."

8. Jack D. L. Holmes, "Indigo in Colonial Louisiana and the Floridas," *Louisiana History*, VIII (Fall, 1967), 329–49. John Clark writes that in addition to the adverse weather conditions between 1791 and 1793, "dampness seems to have been the most serious problem because indigo requires a fairly dry climate," in *New Orleans, 1718–1812: An Economic History*, 188.

9. France was surrounded by a hostile Europe during the wars of the French Revolution, and she even became involved in a period of quasi-war with the United States, 1797–1800. Louisiana colonists continued to hope for the return of French sovereignty, and this wish was encouraged by the knowledge that such was one of the subjects of negotiation between the great powers at this time. See, for example, the accounts discussed by: Mildred S. Fletcher, "Louisiana as a Factor in French Diplomacy from 1763 to 1800," *Mississippi Valley Historical Review*, XVII (December, 1930), 367–76; E. Wilson Lyon, *Louisiana in French Diplomacy, 1759–1804* (2nd ed.; Norman, 1974); and DeConde, *This Affair of Louisiana*, 75–105.

10. On the subject of the Louisiana expedition prepared by Napoleon Bonaparte, see: Ronald D. Smith, "Napoleon and Louisiana: Failure of the Proposed Expedition to Occupy and Defend Louisiana, 1801–1803," *Louisiana History*, XII (1971), 21–40; and Robert D. Bush, "Colonial Administration in French Louisiana: The Napoleonic Episode, 1802–1803," *Publications of the Louisiana Historical Society*, series 2, II (1975), 36–59.

11. Lower Louisiana is situated on about the same degree of latitude as Egypt, which includes Alexandria and Cairo. Its physical geography therefore had a similarity with Egypt, and New Orleans with Alexandria. Napoleon's famous Egyptian campaign of 1798 resulted in some spectacular publicity for him, and the fascination with this region remained in French popular opinion for some time—despite Admiral Nelson's destruction of the French fleet anchored in Aboukir Bay!

12. James Pitot's journey to the East Coast via the Natchez Trace and the Ohio Valley allowed him to gain firsthand knowledge regarding Indian tribes along his route; see Pitot, *Documentary Study*, 38.

CHAPTER ONE

1. See the report prepared by General Georges Victor Collot, *Voyage dans l'Amérique septentrionale ou description des pays opposés par le Mississippi, l'Ohio, le Missouri, et autres rivières affluentes. . . .* (Paris, 1826). Collot had served in the West Indies prior to his travels in the United States from 1796–1797, and copies of his report circulated in government circles until it was published postumously in 1826.

2. By the term government James Pitot means the civil and military affairs administered directly by the governor; finances were handled by the intendant, who was the fiscal agent of the king and responsible for assessing and collecting all revenues in the colony. Like the French colonial administration before 1789, Spanish colonial government was a dualistic system with civilian and military officials. The intendant's power and his autonomy derived from his exclusive control over customs, taxes, and duties. This explains why the Spanish intendant, Juan Ventura Morales, could revoke the right of deposit for Americans at New Orleans in 1802–1803 without either the prior knowledge of or interference by the governor, Don Juan Manuel de Salcedo. The order came directly from the king to Morales.

3. Writing these *Observations* in the latter part of 1801 and in the spring of 1802, James Pitot had been a resident of Louisiana since August, 1796.

4. Don Francisco Luis Héctor, born François Louis, Barón de Carondelet, was governor of Louisiana from 1791 to 1797, and was the only Spanish administrator for whom James Pitot could find positive merits in either his professional or personal life.

5. The reference is to the wars of the French Revolution that involved several of the European powers in coalitions against France. The particular case described at this point refers to Spain's participation in the First Coalition from March 1793 until she withdrew from the anti-French coalition by signing a separate peace at Basel (July 22, 1795). Again, Pitot refers to the implication of international revolution by the Jacobins that permeated the colony at this time.

6. By the terms of the Treaty of Basel (July 22, 1795), Spain transferred its colony of Santo Domingo to France, after the latter had sought unsuccessfully to obtain Lousiana. See Whitaker, *Spanish-American Frontier*, 205.

7. The most famous example of anti-Spanish secret activities plotted by the

French representative in the United States was that by Citizen Edmond Charles Génet, French Minister in Philadelphia. See the description in Alexander DeConde, *Entangling Alliances* (Durham, 1958), 197–203. A good analysis of Spain's reaction to these events and her own defense plans is provided by Abraham P. Nasatir, *Spanish War Vessels on the Mississippi, 1792–1796* (New Haven, 1968).

8. James Pitot's *Observations* reflects a contemporary dilemma for the Louisiana colonist-planter of this era. On the one hand they desperately needed Negroes to work in the fields in order to harvest sugarcane and cotton, the new means to their prosperity. On the other hand, they were panic-stricken with the thought that the Negroes would become infected with the Saint-Domingue revolutionary plague and would rise up against them. On the subject of Spanish policy regarding the slave trade, see Royal Decree of His Majesty conceding freedom for the commerce of Negroes (1791), in the Historic New Orleans Collection.

9. Jack D. L. Holmes maintains that the Pointe Coupée incident was hatched, according to the popular view, by Governor Carondelet in order to destroy his opposition, see "The Abortive Slave Revolt at Point Coupée," *Louisiana History*, XI (Fall 1970), 348.

10. A Franco-Spanish alliance followed the Treaty of Basel which was directed against Great Britain, the historic enemy of both powers and the one country whose vast global empire threatened Spanish possessions in the New World.

11. Carondelet held both the office of intendant and governor in Louisiana from 1792 to 1794. An example of his administration from this era is his "Proclamation on Good Government . . ." (January 26, 1792), in the Historic New Orleans Collection.

12. Notably the Carondelet Canal, later known as the Old Basin Canal, which provided a waterway from Bayou St. John to a turning basin located at the present site of the Municipal Auditorium in New Orleans.

13. The issue of exact boundary lines for the colony of Louisiana was the subject of much negotiation among French, Spanish, English, and American representatives. See, for example, the description in DeConde, *This Affair of Louisiana*, 169–71; Also, the relevant documents, 1795–1804, *Laussat Papers*, Historic New Orleans Collection; and Appendix I, articles II and IV.

14. Carondelet was appointed president of the Royal Audience of the province of Quito, now Ecuador, and he left Louisiana in the fall of 1797.

15. Manuel Gayoso de Lemos, commandant of the Natchez District, succeeded Carondelet and arrived in New Orleans in August, 1797. His career as governor of Louisiana is described by Jack D. L. Holmes, *Gayoso: The Life of a Spanish Governor in the Mississippi Valley, 1789–1799* (Baton Rouge, 1965).

16. Spain, facing a hostile England, needed a friendly or at least a neutral neighbor in America following her change in alliances in 1795; this and the failure of her frontiers dispute with the United States were among the reasons for her concessions in the Treaty of San Lorenzo (October 27, 1795), also known as the Pinckney Treaty. See the history of this interesting document as provided by Samuel Flagg Bemis, *Pinckney's Treaty: America's Advantage from Europe's Distress, 1783–1800.* (New Haven, 1965), and the text of the document in Appendix I.

17. The Treaty of San Lorenzo gave the United States the right of free navigation of the Mississippi River, and a place of deposit at New Orleans, thereby setting the stage for the controversy that was to erupt in 1802–1803 when Juan Ventura Morales, the Spanish intendant, withdrew this provision upon secret

instructions from Spain. See Appendix I, Article XXII.

18. DeConde, *This Affair of Louisiana*, 69, 70, 71, 93, 94, 99, 108, 216.

19. Pitot's reference at this point is to the Franco-Spanish hostilities from 1793 to 1795.

20. For example, the plot that involved General James Wilkinson, among others, to invade Louisiana via Natchez; see the description provided by Whitaker, *Mississippi Question*, 116–19, 124.

21. According to Whitaker, Andrew Ellicott, the American commissioner at Natchez during Governor Gayoso's administration, was the person who urged the settlers to abandon Spain, in *Mississippi Question*, 61. Throughout this long discourse on American ambitions toward Louisiana, it ought not to be forgotten that Pitot himself was a naturalized American citizen—a fact which he did not disclose to French officials.

22. James Pitot left New Orleans in early August, 1798, and began the trip to the United States that took him through Natchez: Pitot, *Documentary Study*, 38. General Wilkinson arrived in Natchez on August 20, 1798: D. Clayton James, *Antebellum Natchez* (Baton Rouge, 1968), 76.

23. A state of quasi-war existed between France and the United States from 1797 to 1800, and this hostility resulted in legislation in Congress such as the Alien and Sedition Acts directed against suspected hostile agents of a foreign power. The problem is discussed by Alexander DeConde, *The Quasi-War* (New York, 1966).

24. James Pitot returned to New Orleans in May, 1799.

25. Charles Gayarré first popularized this story, in *History of Louisiana: The Spanish Domination* (2nd ed.; New Orleans: 1879), III, 405; Jack D. L. Holmes, however, takes exception to it in *Gayoso*, 265–66.

26. Colonel William Blount was a United States senator from Tennessee, and a former governor of that territory before its admission to the Union; he was also a land speculator. See Isaac Joslin Cox (ed.), "Documents on the Blount Conspiracy, 1795–1797," *American Historical Review*, X (1905), 574–606.

27. See the following: William Augustus Bowles, *Authentic Memoirs of William Augustus Bowles, Esquire, Ambassador from the United Nations of Creeks and Cherokees to the Court of London* (London: R. Foulder, 1791), 79 pages; Elisha Douglass, "The Adventurer Bowles," *William And Mary Quarterly*, 2nd ser., VI (1949), 3–23; Lawrence Kinnaird, "The Significance of William Augustus Bowles' Seizure of Panton's Apalachee Store in 1792," *Florida Historical Quarterly*, IX (1931), 156–92; and Pierre Clément de Laussat, *Memoirs of My Life*, trans. Agnes-Josephine Pastwa (Baton Rouge, 1978), 36–39.

28. For a discussion of the opposition to Spanish policy regarding trade regulations in Louisiana, see Clark, *New Orleans, 1718–1812: An Economic History*, 242. Also of interest on this subject is Gilbert C. Din, "Spain's Immigration Policy in Louisiana and the American Penetration, 1792–1803," *Southwestern Historical Quarterly*, LXXVI (1973), 255–76.

29. Francisco Bouligny assumed charge of military forces; Nicolas Maria Vidal, the political and civil government as auditor; and, Juan Ventura Morales, judicial and financial affairs as intendant.

30. Sebastian Calvo de la Puerto y O'Farril, Marques de Casa Calvo.

31. See the description in Whitaker, *Mississippi Question*, 167; and the map illustrations.

32. Don Juan Manuel de Salcedo arrived in New Orleans as governor of Louisiana in June, 1801.

33. Piastre was the colonial name for the Spanish medium of exchange; the

gourde was the denomination used in Saint-Domingue, where James Pitot had lived for several years. The piastre was acutally the peso fuerte, a silver coin minted in Mexico and worth about one American dollar at the time; the gourde was also worth about one American dollar in exchange, so that the two terms are actually redundant here.

34. For a description of the depreciation of paper money in Louisiana from 1795 to 1800, see Clark, *New Orleans, 1718–1812: An Economic History*, 267–69.
35. The benefit worked as follows: by taking hard money, or specie, from the treasury and using it to acquire the depreciated local paper money, debts could then be repaid at a tremendous savings; and if the creditor objected, he was forced to legal recourse against officials of the very government personnel who were defrauding him!
36. *Pacotilles* were small amounts of merchandise carried on shipboard by sailors or individuals, which they sold at debarkation.

CHAPTER TWO

1. James Pitot was himself elected as a ward commissioner on January 8, 1802. He did not appear before the city government to accept the position until May 27, 1802, and then left immediately for France. Pitot, *Documentary Study*, 38–39.
2. Bayou St. John. John G. Clark writes that "by 1803 the canal, useless except for very small craft, was an open sewer running the width of the city," in *New Orleans, 1718–1812: An Economic History*, 291. Also Laussat, *Memoirs*, 25–27.

CHAPTER THREE

1. Antoine Crozat in 1712 and then John Law in 1717, both had been given exclusive monopoly concessions in Louisiana by the French crown; Spain did not resort to this form of administration in Louisiana. However, the Panton, Leslie Company held a virtual monopoly on the Indian trade from their base at Pensacola, and it was this special arrangement that mystified James Pitot.
2. The peace treaty signed in Paris on February 10, 1763, ended the Seven Years' War in Europe, and resulted in Britain's domination of North America. Jean Jacques d'Abbadie arrived in New Orleans on June 29, 1763. Great Britain controlled West Florida and kept it from 1763 until she lost it as a result of Spanish participation in the War of American Independence, after which, in 1783, it was returned to Spain. See the "Glossary of Eighteenth-Century Mercantile Terms," in Margaret Fisher Dalrymple (ed.), *The Merchant of Manchac: The Letterbooks of John Fitzpatrick, 1768–1790* (Baton Rouge, 1978), 433–35.
3. Jean Jacques d'Abbadie died in February 1765, and was succeeded by Charles Philippe Aubry, who commanded the French military garrison at New Orleans. Antonio de Ulloa, the first Spanish governor, arrived in Louisiana in March, 1766. Don Alexander O'Reilly was the second Spanish governor who arrived in 1769.
4. For a brief summary of the problem, see Clark, *New Orleans, 1718–1812: An Economic History*. 140–41.
5. James Pitot and his partner, Jean Lanthois, managed trading vessels on the Mississippi River in 1797; see the account provided by Pitot, *Documentary, Study*, 37–38.
6. During the American Revolution, Spain joined the anti-British coalition in 1779. Spain's governor of Louisiana, Don Bernardo de Gálvez, won the Gulf

Coast from British control, thereby establishing a strong hand for Spanish diplomats at the peace conference in 1783. Britain's cost for peace with Spain was therefore territorial concessions in Florida, although British merchants and privateers continued to intrude into Spanish waters thereafter.

7. Spain had imposed an export duty of 6 percent and an import duty of 15 percent; hence, the duty on imports from the American settlements up river was 15 percent until reduced to 6 percent in 1793. See Clark, *New Orleans, 1718–1812: An Economic History*, 238; Whitaker, *Spanish-American Frontier*, 176, 193. See the tariff schedule, Appendix II.

8. Carondelet acted under orders from Madrid (October 29, 1796) delaying the evacuation of Natchez, but several months after Governor Gayoso took office, he was ordered to turn Natchez over to the United States immediately. The boundary line in question was that of the thirty-first parallel. See the description in DeConde, *This Affair of Louisiana*, 61–62; and the text in Appendix I, Article IV.

9. Spanish shipping in the Gulf of Mexico and Caribbean was directly proportional to its convoy protection for success, and such protection was always in short supply as James Pitot laments. British privateers, operating out of New Providence Island in the British West Indies, frustrated the regular traffic between Spain's colonies, and frightened neutral merchants from shipping goods to them. Even river pirates were a problem, which the Spanish river fleet attempted to correct.

10. Juan Ventura Morales first arrived in Louisiana as a clerk in the entourage of Governor Gálvez; he served as intendant in 1784–1785, 1796–1800, and finally from 1801–1803.

11. Ramon Lopez y Angullo was intendant from January 1, 1800 to July 13, 1801.

12. James Pitot is referring here to the rumors of the peace settlement to be concluded (March 27, 1802) between France and England in the Peace of Amiens. The best general discussion of the complicated treaty arrangements by France, Spain, and the United States is that by DeConde, *This Affair of Louisiana*, 91–105.

13. The three French ports were: Bordeaux, Rouen, and St. Malo.

14. Without an officially encouraged export trade between Louisiana and other countries whereby the colony could pay for her imports, those persons who wished to trade here had to resort to a variety of means. The most chronic form of trading in Louisiana, and which avoided the duties, was that of smuggling. As a result, a rather elaborate and sophisticated smuggling trade developed, which later caused American officials as much trouble as it had done for their Spanish predecessors.

CHAPTER FOUR

1. The original cession of Louisiana was made by the French government in a treaty of November 3, 1762, although the first Spanish administrator did not arrive in the colony until 1766. Much to the chagrin of the colonists, they discovered that they were pawns in the international relations of the great powers in Europe.

2. A delegation of French inhabitants from Louisiana went to Paris in order to appeal to Louis XV not to cede the colony to Spain. Despite its transfer, the colony remained French in its cultural tradition throughout the years of Spanish control, and this looking to France by the colonists was partially responsible for the abortive Creole rebellion of 1769. The first turbulent years of Spanish Louisiana are well documented by John Preston Moore, *Revolt in*

Louisiana: The Spanish Occupation, 1766–1770 (Baton Rouge, 1976).

3. Don Luis de Unzaga was confirmed as governor of Louisiana on August 17, 1772.

4. The Panton, Leslie Company of Pensacola had control of the Indiana trade since 1785; the privileges extended as far as the Chickasaw Bluffs, at Memphis, on the Mississippi River, and the whole of the Gulf Coast area. See Marie Taylor Greenslade, "William Panton" and "The Panton, Leslie Papers," *Florida Historical Quarterly*, XIV (1935), 107–32. Among the archives at the Historic New Orleans Collection is an interesting policy statement on Indian affairs by Governor Gayoso (April 19, 1798) to the commandant at Mobile, sixteen pages in Spanish.

5. Etienne de Boré was the "active and enterprising planter" referred to; Antonio Mendez had planted sugarcane "the year before"; and Antonio Morin was the sugarmaker. John Clark estimates that sugar production per Negro slave was about 3,000 pounds, in *New Orleans, 1718–1812: An Economic History*, 219.

6. While the exchange rates for currencies used in Louisiana varied, the conversion in 1802 was as follows: the piastre was about equal to one American dollar; the piastre was equal to five livres tournois, which in turn was subdivided into 20 sols tournois or approximately one cent each. Thus, the reference here to 50 sols tournois per pound would be about 50 cents per pound.

7. James Pitot became an American citizen in Philadelphia in 1796 and immediately came to New Orleans in order to take advantage of the favorable terms offered Americans in the Treaty of San Lorenzo. See the discussion by R. Carmelo Arena, "Philadelphia—Spanish New Orleans Trade in the 1790s," *Louisiana History*, III (Fall, 1961), 429–45.

CHAPTER FIVE

1. These officials were Juan Ventura Morales, Jose Martinez de la Pedrera, and Nicholas Maria Vidal.

CHAPTER SIX

1. Barthélemy Lafon, architect, engineer, cartographer, and militia officer from New Orleans. A tracing of the map was found in 1966 in the archives of the Service Historique de l'Armée at Vincennes. There are actually two maps: (1) "Carte du Mississipi et des ses Branches" and (2) "Carte d'une partie de la Basse Louisiane et de la Floride Occidentale." The second is a portion of the first map, drawn to a larger scale.

2. St. Marks, Florida, which was captured by Bowles, but then retaken by the Spaniards in June, 1800.

3. See the Map of the Mississippi and Its Branches.

4. The islands beginning at Mobile Bay and running westward are Dauphin, Petit Bois, Horn, Ship, and Cat Islands.

5. See the Map of a Portion of Lower Louisiana and Western Florida.

6. Fort Saint Philip at Plaquemines.

7. On the subject of early settlements in Louisiana, see: Marcel Giraud, *A History of French Louisiana*, trans. Joseph C. Lambert (4 vols.; Baton Rouge, 1974), I; and Jay Higginbotham, *Old Mobile, Fort Louis de la Louisiane, 1702–1711* (Mobile, 1977).

8. The reference is to the plantation in Saint Bernard Parish, not the present-day

Gentilly Section of the city of New Orleans.

9. From Saint John the Baptist Parish to the mouth of the Mississippi River.

10. For a description of the *chênière*, see Betsy Swanson, *Historic Jefferson Parish from Shore to Shore* (Gretna, 1975), 18, 19.

11. The unit of land measurement common in much of Louisiana. The arpent is "less than an acre, 605 arpents being equal to 512 acres," and is also used as a unit of lineal measure "roughly equal to 192 feet," in William A. Read, *Louisiana-French* (Baton Rouge, 1931), 3.

12. The exact location is: 29° 56′ 57″ latitude, by 90° 04′ 11″ longitude. The word *quarré* is old French for *carré*. James Pitot uses it for the entire city of New Orleans in 1802.

13. Islets are city blocks, a term that was applied generally in New Orleans, as it was also in the French West Indies.

14. Formerly known as the *Place d'Armes*, the site is now known as Jackson Square.

15. Beginning at Canal Street and the river, and going clockwise they were Fort Saint Louis, Fort Burgundy, Fort Saint John, Fort Saint Charles. There was also at one time Fort Saint Ferdinand, which was located between Fort Burgundy and Fort Saint John, at what is now the corner of Rampart and Saint Anne streets.

16. Faubourg Sainte Marie, bounded by what is now Common Street, the Mississippi River, Howard Avenue, and Rampart Street.

17. The area below Esplanade Avenue, later known as the Faubourg Marigny.

18. Andres Almonester y Roxas

19. The term refers to the members of the *cabildo*, or town council, and also to the building in which they met. See John G. Clark, "The Role of the City Government in the Economic Development of New Orleans: Cabildo and City Council, 1783–1812," in McDermott, *The Spanish in the Mississippi Valley*, 133–48.

20. Under the Spanish system in Louisiana, judges used their residences instead of courtrooms in office buildings as found throughout the United States.

21. James Pitot is referring to the Ursuline nuns brought to Louisiana for the education of the girls. The Ignoratine brother, a term used opprobriously, designated a member of the Brothers of the Christian Schools.

22. The Carondelet Canal was later to be called the Old Basin Canal.

23. James Pitot served as president and a director of the Orleans Navigation Company for several years, which undertook to complete this project but never did. See Clark, *New Orleans, 1718–1812: An Economic History*, Table VIII, 293; Pitot, *Documentary Study*, 85–88.

24. The First and Second German Parishes are now Saint Charles Parish and Saint John the Baptist Parish. For the locations of the bayous and points referred to, see the maps and text found in Edwin Adams Davis (ed.), *The Rivers and Bayous of Louisiana* (Baton Rouge, 1968).

25. Galvestown was settled by American and English refugees from British West Florida around 1778. It was located near the junction of Bayou Manchac and the Amite River. Galvestown was an important outpost during the American Revolutionary War activities in Louisiana (1779–1781) and was later incorporated into neighboring communities after 1809.

26. Saint James Parish.

27. Assumption Parish plus what is now Lafourche Parish. The parish of Manchac is now Ascension and Iberville parishes.

28. Bayou Lafourche flows into the Gulf of Mexico between what is called Caminada Bay and Timbalier Bay.

29. An "island" bounded by Lake Borgne, Lake Pontchartrain, the Iberville River, and the Mississippi River.
30. The reference here is to Spanish involvement in the War of the American Revolution (1779–1783), not the French Revolutionary struggles.
31. The right of navigation on the Mississippi was virtually an open door through which an unbounded smuggling trade operated, and which was a very acceptable profession involving the more enterprising merchants of New Orleans.
32. The issue of boundaries between Pensacola and the Mississippi River areas north of the Iberville River plagued the diplomatic negotiations throughout this era. Since they were claimed by the British as part of their territory in West Florida, and also by the Spanish, the French and then the Americans, the area in question was simply referred to as the Florida Parishes. See Isaac J. Cox, *The West Florida Controversy, 1798–1813* (Baitimore, 1918); and, on the problems of navigation on the Iberville River, Philip Pittman, *The Present State of the European Settlements on the Mississippi* (Cleveland, 1906), 69–70.
33. The port of Lake Charles, Louisiana, is presently located on th Calcasieu River about forty miles from the Gulf.
34. The name Cados Mountains is a reference to the Rocky Mountains, possibly named for the Caddos Indians (the name Cadodaquis Tribe appears on early French maps), who lived along the Red River, but not as far as Santa Fe. (Map makers often named geographical places or locations for the Indian tribe or tribes known to inhabit these unexplored areas.) James Pitot assumed that the Red River had its origin in the area of the Spanish settlement of Santa Fe. Exact descriptions and maps of this area were chronically inaccurate because of the great distances involved, hostile Indian tribes in the area, and lack of reliable information in New Orleans regarding this area administered by the viceroy of Mexico.
35. This abrupt ending of the topographical description leaves several unanswered questions. Did James Pitot intend to end his *Observations* here? Or were some of the pages from the original manuscript lost?

Bibliography

ARCHIVES

Archives de la Ville du Havre, Le Havre
Archives Départementales de la Gironde, Bordeaux
Archives Départementales de la Manche, Saint-Lô
Archives Nationales, Paris
Bibliothèque Nationale, Paris
The Historic New Orleans Collection, New Orleans
Howard-Tilton Library Special Collections, Tulane University, New Orleans
Louisiana Division, New Orleans Public Library, New Orleans
Service Historique de l'Armée, Vincennes

ARTICLES

Arena, R. Camelo. "Philadelphia-Spanish New Orleans Trade in the 1790s." *Louisiana History*, III, (Fall, 1961), 429–45.
Bush, Robert D. "Colonial Administration in French Louisiana: The Napoleonic Episode, 1802–1803." *Publications of the Louisiana Historical Society*, Series 2, II (1975), 36–59.
Carrigan, Jo Ann. "The Pestilence of 1796—New Orleans First Officially Recorded Yellow Fever Epidemic." *McNeese Review*, XIII (1962), 27–36.
Cox, Isaac Joslin, ed. "Documents on the Blount Conspiracy, 1795–1797." *American Historical Review*, X (1905), 574–606.
Din, Gilbert C. "Spain's Immigration Policy in Louisiana and the American Penetration, 1792–1803." *Southwestern Historical Quarterly*, LXXVI (1973), 255–76.
Douglas, Elisha P. "The Adventurer Bowles." *William And Mary Quarterly*, 2nd ser., VI (1949), 3–23.
Fletcher, Mildred S. "Louisiana as a Factor in French Diplomacy from 1763 to 1800." *Mississippi Valley Historical Review*, XVII (December, 1930), 367–76.
Gardeur, René J. Le, and Henry C. Pitot. "An Unpublished Memoir of Spanish Louisiana, 1796–1802." In John Francis McDermott, ed. *Frenchmen and French Ways in the Mississippi Valley*. Urbana: University of Illinois Press, 1969, pp. 73–86.

191

Bibliography

Greenslade, Marie Taylor. "William Panton" and "The Panton, Leslie Papers."
Florida Historical Quarterly, XIV (1935), 107–32.
Holmes, Jack D. L. "The Abortive Slave Revolt at Point Coupée." *Louisiana History*,
XI (Fall, 1970), 341–62.
――――. "Indigo in Colonial Louisiana and the Floridas." *Louisiana History*, VIII
(Fall, 1967), 329–49.
――――. "Some Economic Problems of Spanish Governors in Louisiana." *Hispanic
American Historical Review*, XLII (November, 1962), 521–43.
Kinnaird, Lawrence. "The Significance of William Augustus Bowles' Seizure of
Panton's Apalachee Store in 1792." *Florida Historical Quarterly*, IX (1931), 156–92.
Liljegren, Ernest R. "Jacobinism in Spanish Louisiana, 1792–1797." *Louisiana
Historical Quarterly*, XXII (January, 1939), 47–97.
Sterling, David Lee, ed. "New Orleans, 1801: An Account by John Pintard."
Louisiana Historical Quarterly, XXXIV (July, 1951), 217–33.
Whitaker, Arthur P. "The Commerce of Louisiana and the Floridas at the End of
the Eighteenth Century." *Hispanic American Historical Review*, VIII (May, 1928),
190–203.
――――. "Spain and the Retrocession of Louisiana." *American Historical Review*,
XXXIX (1934), 454–76.

BOOKS

Bemis, Samuel Flagg. *Pinckney's Treaty: America's Advantage from Europe's Distress,
1783–1800*. New Haven: Yale University Press, 1965.
Berquin-Duvallon, Pierre Louis. *Vue de la colonia espagnole du Mississipi ou des
provinces de Louisiane et Floride Occidentale en l'année 1802, par un observateur résident
sur les lieux*. Paris: A l'Imprimerie Expéditive, 1803.
Clark, John G. *New Orleans, 1718–1812: An Economic History*. Baton Rouge: Louisi-
ana State University Press, 1970.
Collot, George Henri Victor. *Voyage dans l'Amérique septentrionale ou description des
pays opposés par le Mississipi, l'Ohio, le Missouri, et autres rivières affluentes.* . . . Paris:
A. Bertrand, 1826.
Cox, Isaac J., ed. *The West Florida Controversy, 1798–1813*. Baltimore: Johns
Hopkins University Press, 1918.
Dalrymple, Margaret Fisher, ed. *The Merchant of Manchac: The Letterbooks of John
Fitzpatrick, 1768–1790*. Baton Rouge: Louisiana State University Press, 1978.
Davis, Edwin Adams, ed. *The Rivers and Bayous of Louisiana*. Baton Rouge: Louisi-
ana Education Research Association, 1968.
DeConde, Alexander. *Entangling Alliances*. Durham: Duke University Press, 1958.
――――. *The Quasi-War*. New York: Charles Scribner's Sons, 1966.
――――. *This Affair of Louisiana*. New York: Charles Scribner's Sons, 1976.
Gayarré, Charles. *History of Louisiana: The Spanish Domination*. 2nd ed. Vol. III. New
Orleans: Gresham, 1879.
Giraud, Marcel. *A History of French Louisiana*. Translated by Joseph C. Lambert. 4
vols. Baton Rouge: Louisiana State University Press, 1974.
Higganbotham, Jay. *Old Mobile, Fort Louis de la Louisiane, 1702–1711*. Mobile, Ala.:
Museum of the city of Mobile, 1977.
Holmes, Jack D. L. *Gayoso: The Life of a Spanish Governor in the Mississippi Valley,
1789–1799*. Baton Rouge: Louisiana State University Press, 1965.
――――. *A Guide to Spanish Louisiana, 1762–1806*. New Orleans: Louisiana Collection
Series, 1970.
James, D. Clayton. *Antebellum Natchez*. Baton Rouge: Louisiana State University
Press, 1968.
King, Grace. *Creole Families of New Orleans*. New York: Macmillan, 1921.

Bibliography

Kinnard, Lawrence, ed. *Annual Report of the American Historical Association for the Year 1945, Spain in the Mississippi Valley, 1765–1794.* 3 vols. Washington: U.S. Government Printing Office, 1946.

Kniffen, Fred B. *The Indians of Louisiana.* Gretna, La.: Pelican Publishing Co., 1976.

Laussat, Pierre Clément de. *Memoirs of My Life.* Translated by Agnes-Josephine Pastwa. Baton Rouge: Louisiana State University Press, 1978.

Lyon, E. Wilson, *Louisiana in French Diplomacy, 1759–1804.* Norman: University of Oklahoma Press, 1934.

Martin, François-Xavier, *The History of Louisiana from the Earliest Period.* 3rd ed. Gretna, La.: Pelican Publishing Co., 1975.

McDermott, John Francis, ed. *Frenchmen and French Ways in the Mississippi Valley.* Urbana: University of Illinois Press, 1969.

——. *The Spanish in the Mississippi Valley, 1762–1804.* Urbana: University of Illinois Press, 1974.

Miller, David Hunter, ed. *Treaties and Other International Acts of the United States.* 8 vols. Washington: U.S. Government Printing Office, 1931–1948.

Moore, John Preston. *Revolt in Louisiana: The Spanish Occupation, 1766–1770.* Baton Rouge: Louisiana State University Press, 1976.

Nasatir, Abraham P. *Spanish War Vessels on the Mississippi, 1792–1796.* New Haven: Yale University Press, 1968.

Oudard, Georges. *Vieille Amérique: La Louisiane au temps des français.* Paris: Plon, 1931.

Pitot, Henry Clement. *James Pitot (1761–1831): A Documentry Study.* New Orleans: Bocage Books, 1968.

Pittman, Philip. *The Present State of the European Settlements on the Mississippi.* Cleveland: Arthur H. Clark, 1906.

Read, William A. *Louisiana-French.* Baton Rouge: Louisiana State University Press, 1931.

Swanson, Betsy. *Historic Jefferson Parish from Shore to Shore.* Gretna, La.: Pelican Publishing Co., 1975.

Whitaker, Arthur Preston. *The Mississippi Question, 1795–1803: A Study in Trade, Politics and Diplomacy.* New York: D. Appleton-Century Crofts, 1934.

——. *The Spanish-American Frontier, 1783–1795: The Westward Movement and the Spanish Retreat in the Mississippi Valley.* New York: Houghton Mifflin, 1927.

Index

199